W9-BYG-652

RISE

TO THE

TOP

RISE
TO THE
TOP

How Women Leverage Their
Professional Persona to Earn More

Stacey Hawley

POQUOSON PUBLIC LIBRARY
500 CITY HALL AVE
POQUOSON, VA 23662

CAREER
PRESS

Pompton Plains, N.J.

Copyright © 2015 by Stacey Hawley

All rights reserved under the Pan-American and International Copyright Conventions. This book may not be reproduced, in whole or in part, in any form or by any means electronic or mechanical, including photocopying, recording, or by any information storage and retrieval system now known or hereafter invented, without written permission from the publisher, The Career Press.

RISE TO THE TOP
EDITED AND TYPESET BY KARA KUMPEL
Cover design by Joanna Williams Design
Printed in the U.S.A.

To order this title, please call toll-free 1-800-CAREER-1 (NJ and Canada: 201-848-0310) to order using VISA or MasterCard, or for further information on books from Career Press.

The Career Press, Inc.
220 West Parkway, Unit 12
Pompton Plains, NJ 07444
www.careerpress.com

Library of Congress Cataloging-in-Publication Data
Hawley, Stacey.
    Rise to the top : how woman leverage their professional per-sona to earn more and rise to the top / Stacey Hawley.
        pages cm
    Includes bibliographical references and index.
    ISBN 978-1-60163-333-0 (paperback) -- ISBN 978-1-60163-453-5 (ebook) 1. Women executives--United States. 2. Pay equity--United States. 3. Executives--Salaries, etc.--United States. 4. Women--Employment--United States. I. Title.

    HD6054.4.U6H39 2014
    331.4'8165800973--dc23

                                                            2014009337

*To my mother, the woman who gave me
the greatest gift of all: courage.*

Acknowledgments

Imagine climbing the corporate ladder. As a woman. Thirty years ago. *Painful, humiliating, lonely, rewarding, eye-opening, commendable*, and *brave* are a few words that come to mind.

Many of today's opportunities exist because of courageous trailblazers. It is impossible to truly understand the frustrations and obstacles faced by the women who created the abundant opportunities available today. Thank you to the thousands of powerhouse personalities who pave the way for other women every day. These women constantly encourage me to grow, lead, and persevere, either through example or instruction. Thank you for opening the doors for other women to forge their career paths and rise to the top.

My personal life has been filled with amazing powerhouse personalities who taught me to persist. My grandmothers and mother immigrated to the United States from Greece to create a better life for their families. My mother was the first child in her family to attend college, and, even more courageous, attended school in her 30s while raising two kids because she wanted to pursue a new career. I am also grateful for my mother-in-law, my godmother, aunts, and sisters who are blazing their own trails for themselves and for others to follow.

Friends are a powerhouse's best support system. I have been blessed with two dear women who support and challenge me in both my professional and personal life. Their unwavering support undoubtedly led to this book's creation. Thank you, Melissa and Chris, for not allowing me to give up, for challenging me, and for always supporting me.

"Growing up" at Towers exposed me to many amazing professionals. Thank you to Adrienne, who taught me "it is just as important to learn what *not* to do as it is to learn what to do," and Rob, who shared the best piece of advice ever: "If you believe something of yourself, that is how others will perceive you. Perception is 90 percent of reality." And thank you to Linda, my "work mom" who took me under her wing and helped me understand the different powerhouses in our own company.

Every client I met and worked diligently to help succeed became a true friend for me. I learned from each woman's experiences, leadership, and wisdom. Specifically, thank you Pat and Sharon for unknowingly being my mentors and role models. I documented and imitated everything you shared and taught.

This book is a labor of love—a manifestation of my passion to share with women everything I have learned about pay to help them succeed. Robin shared this passion with me and helped promote my passion. Thank you, Robin.

Finally, I have been blessed to marry a true partner and friend. He allows me to try, try, and try some more, encourages me to succeed, and also shows me how to look at things in different ways and from different points of view. Thank you to my husband, Sean—my personal powerhouse.

Contents

Introduction

"Perception is 90 percent of reality."
—Unknown

If I asked you to estimate the annual base salary for a CFO position, what number would pop into your head?

$80,000?

$100,000?

$150,000?

What if I said the position is for a public company? What if I added that the company records more than $30 billion in revenues? Or that the company focuses on telecommunication services? Would your number escalate? (It should.)

$200,000?

$325,000?

$500,000?

$1,000,000??

Now what if I claimed the company was a privately held professional services firm with $1 billion in revenues? Did your number shrink? (Again, it should.)

Let's take this discussion further.

What if I added that the CFO (in any scenario) acts as a true business partner, performs exceptionally well, and is highly valued by the organization? Alternatively, how does your thinking change if the person is new to the role, only "meets expectations," and may or may not be highly valued?

The purpose of this exercise was to show that compensation is both *objective* and *subjective*. The objective part involves industry peers, robust data, structures, and guidelines. The subjective part—which highly influences the objective part—is *individual performance and perception*. Performance is measured by achievement against goals, strategic impact to the organization, and how the individual is valued. This performance influence is based on individual perception, which determines the importance of the underlying performance (it isn't all linear—there is a range of gray). This perception then determines the individual's resulting compensation.

Think of it as a math formula:

Compensation = f(x), where f = performance and (x) = perception

Maximizing compensation comes down to:

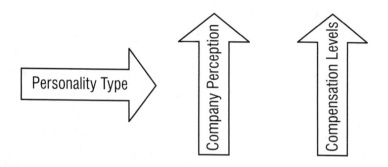

I have witnessed firsthand how perception impacts compensation levels. As an executive compensation consultant, I partner with senior management and boards to develop compensation philosophies and peer groups, review and analyze data, and discuss how to use the data to determine pay levels. For almost two decades now I have worked with companies across many industries at various stages of growth to review, develop, and refine compensation programs. I am at the table. Watching. Listening. Answering questions. Advising. I am part of program discussions, observing how compensation decisions are made using the information that has been provided.

As objective as the process might *try* to be, there is still an element of subjectivity; individuals can influence the outcome. What I have learned, after almost 20 years of helping companies and individuals determine "competitive" and "rewarding" pay programs and levels, is that *how you play the game matters*. There is more to making money than just moving the ball down the field; *how* you move the ball matters. Even if you think you understand the value of a job (in other words, how much a job is worth), that doesn't mean you are going to get it.

Just knowing the value isn't enough. You can't just ask for it. Other people need to believe you are worth it.

Over and over again, women have asked me what I have learned about negotiating pay and dealing with complex situations, and how to leverage my insights. So now I am sharing what I have learned with you. I believe that men are wired differently than women, and therefore play this game better than women. I also believe that women can learn to play the game better. After engaging in intense executive compensation discussions with CEOs, boards, senior leadership, and human resources professionals, I can recognize *when and how* some women are highly valued and *when and how* some women are less highly valued.

I have also learned—and truly believe—that companies (by and large) do the right thing. Companies develop robust compensation practices rooted in data and analyses, and they implement those practices based on established guidelines and structures. Most importantly, companies are not trying to limit women's earning capabilities. In fact, it's quite the opposite. I have had the pleasure of partnering with senior male executives who wholeheartedly advocate for their female counterparts. Furthermore, women have much more control over the process than they realize. And they need to exercise this control. Women can change the playing field and increase their earnings. Women can minimize missteps and improve their probability of scoring. It all comes down to how women are perceived: perception influences the outcome; perception influences your pay. The most important message is this: **You are a powerhouse**.

I encounter all types of women at every level: acting as active board members, performing at the executive level, seeking the executive level, seeking career advancement, or launching their professional careers. Each woman, regardless of her role, career trajectory, or experiences, is a powerhouse. The important thing is to recognize which type of powerhouse you are—which you will discover in Chapter 4—and then to leverage your powerhouse personality appropriately.

Have you ever met an assertive, strong woman who was comfortable sharing her opinions? Did you then meet a woman who, on the surface, seemed quiet, or not as vocal, or even disinterested? Both of these women are powerhouses. The quiet woman might have appeared submissive and weak, but she may have been assessing the players, gathering information, and formulating her approach and opinion.

One of my first client meetings involved a female chief HR officer. She barely spoke. She just nodded as the CEO spoke. I assumed she was more passive. A year later when the CEO retired and a new CEO came on board, she was one of the only executives who wasn't replaced. I realized she wasn't passive. She was smart. Incredibly smart. She had distanced herself from the retiring CEO and aligned herself with the right players to keep her job. She was a powerhouse.

You are a powerhouse. You need to figure out *which* powerhouse and how to leverage that personality to play the game. Play it well, and maximize your earnings.

This book discusses the game, the players, four types of powerhouse personalities, and how to leverage those personalities. The game is compensation. The players include everyone exercising a significant degree of influence over the outcomes. Performance is critical, and measurable against predetermined outcomes, but not all performance is clearly measurable. The individual component leaves room for interpretation. How well the game is played depends on how you—the player—is perceived.

I will share examples of my experience. (Of course, names, places, and other defining characteristics have been masked for confidentiality reasons. The essence of the story is more important than the details.) The stories I will share help to underscore the process and the outcomes.

You need to understand how you are being perceived in order to leverage that perception and earn more money. Understanding which powerhouse personality describes you and how to play the game will provide you with a complete arsenal of tools for maximizing your compensation and earnings potential. After discussing the game, I will reveal how to leverage each powerhouse personality to improve your overall perception and earn more money. I'll also share other important tips, such as how to avoid the pitfalls of each powerhouse personality.

Although I focus on executive compensation (because then I can discuss all the possible reward vehicles and elements companies use), even if you are not an executive, the process for developing and administering compensation is similar at all levels in the organization. Understanding the process for executive compensation provides insight into the full gamut of possible rewards, and it helps you understand that path and trajectory. In other words, if you are an executive, this book is for you. If you are not an executive (yet), this book is *still* for you.

CHAPTER 1

What Is Compensation?

When I entered the compensation consulting world in 1996, I understood very little about executive compensation. I was a newborn; a baby in the consulting world. Based on a single three-credit course I took at Cornell, I believed "compensation" meant base salary structures determined by a points system. In the course, we researched step systems, in which increases are based on tenure rather than performance (for example, everyone gets a 3 percent increase every year no matter what), and studied the assignment of points to jobs. These points determined base salary levels within an organization: the more points a job earned, the higher its pay level. Our professor discussed pay increases based on tenure (for example, in a union environment), and focused entirely on internally based structures.

It was all so...systematic.

And boring.

Post-graduation, I accepted a role as a compensation analyst for Towers Perrin (now Towers Watson). In today's language, Towers Watson is one of the Big 3 HR consulting firms, along with Aon/Hewitt and Mercer. At the time I joined Towers Perrin (TP), bigger was better because of TP's extensive experience (both technical and consulting). Clients wanted to know what other clients you advised that were *just like them*, and a larger client base meant *access*: access to knowledge, access to information, access to data, and access to exciting, challenging, and complex projects. When I first received the job offer, I discussed Towers with my compensation professor. She relayed the firm's reputation: "Towers is where you go to get trained. It is not where you make a career."

I made a career.

Of course, I had no idea who Towers really was relative to its peers or industry. I didn't comprehend what being a *compensation consultant* meant either. (The following chapter explains compensation consulting in depth, which can help you to better understand how your company has arrived at its current compensation philosophy.) I was just overjoyed to have a job offer at a firm I believed was reputable in a role that would provide me a sound basis for starting a career.

My first real life lesson: Compensation is fascinating.

My second real life lesson: Compensation is *very* personal.

My third real life lesson: My Cornell course barely scratched the surface.

Compensation—especially executive compensation—encompasses an entire rewards package, including base salary, annual incentives, long-term incentives (such as stock options and/or restricted stock), deferred compensation, supplemental benefits, supplemental retirement plans, severance, and other perks. In my opinion, the level of these awards should be market- and performance-driven rather than internally determined. Once I started working for Towers, I realized the Cornell course taught a system based on internal job valuation, whereas Towers promoted an external, or market-driven approach.

When I first joined Towers, the line of business, or practice, focused simply on compensation. I became skilled at developing competitive market rates for all types of jobs, at all levels within an organization. I designed salary structures as well as incentive plans. A few years later, the *specialized* executive compensation practice became a separate group within the broader performance management line of business. The lines of business changed regularly; the firm constantly rethought how to deliver services. But at the end of the day, compensation was compensation. How we analyzed data, designed programs, or partnered with clients never changed.

What Is Executive Compensation?

Executive compensation is not a dirty phrase—although it certainly feels like it. It does not mean excessive pay, egregious salaries, or wealth accumulation without performance or accountability. Executive compensation should not conjure images of $14,000 shower curtains, free personal jets, or playing three rounds of golf while stock options are exercised and securely banked in offshore accounts. Nor should images of Enron and paper shredding or Lehman Brothers' cataclysmic collapse cloud your mind. Yet, because media coverage constantly connects executive compensation to malfeasance or negligence, these images are inevitable. History recounts the following story: A company with a significant financial impact on the economy tanks. Shareholders and media target leadership (perhaps rightly so). However, in addition to targeting leadership's *alleged* malfeasance and inability to execute key strategic decisions, people emphasize the greed that motivated their behavior. Of course, other reasons exist, such as economic recessions, government regulation, or market competition, but regardless, the newspaper headlines tout greed.

And greed is bad.

Therefore pay must be curbed.

Once the media pronounces a supposed lack of checks and balances within a firm, government legislators insist changes must be made to prevent such corruption from reoccurring. In addition to industry legislation, Congress passes compensation legislation such as IRC Code 162(m), regarding the deductibility of compensation exceeding $1 million, and Sarbanes-Oxley, which included penalties for retrieving compensation payments awarded due to malfeasance.

The intent is to curb pay. In time, however, compensation levels inevitably increase. Fortunately, the designs of compensation philosophies—and particularly bonus plans—evolve to more properly ensure that key financial objectives are achieved before payouts are delivered, or that clawback provisions, in which the company takes *back* its money, are securely in place.

Executive compensation—*all* compensation, in fact—can and should be about transparency, accountability, and performance. If companies do not want their programs or actions splashed on the front page of the *Wall Street Journal*, then they shouldn't implement them.

Throughout my tenure as a consultant, I was reassured and refreshed to find individuals motivated to build a company, launch groundbreaking products, expand a business, merge with another company, or divest a product line or service. For most people, *greed* is good: the *greed* to grow and expand. The *greed* to develop new ideas and products. The *greed* to venture into new markets, new industries, or new partnerships. And the *greed* to generate wealth for *others*.

> We had one client who hired us to determine how to reallocate a high portion of the CEO's pay to the employees! The CEO wanted to redistribute the wealth. The tricky part was delivering the compensation without triggering tax burdens to the CEO.

Because I began my career in New York City in the mid-1990s for companies like Prudential, Sony, and Time Warner, I envisioned executives as at least middle-aged, wearing suits and ties, and acting formal in their approach and decision-making.

My fourth real life lesson: That was not the case.

Who Are the Executives?

Executives come in all shapes and sizes. Some companies delineate several levels of executives, and others only define one or two levels of executives, with a few individuals manning each executive role. Factors such as industry and company growth stage impact who companies include in their executive pools.

I learned that not every big fish is an executive; not every big role is an executive role. Thankfully, broadbased compensation—pay programs provided to employees below the executive level—proved easier to define. Companies typically employ a few compensation reward vehicles for the majority of their employees. At the executive level, more vehicles come into play. But before defining the executive compensation program, companies must identify, or define, their executives. What is an executive? What makes an executive? Is it based on scope of responsibility, P&L responsibility, or impact or influence on company strategy?

> *One client, an Internet-based media subsidiary, struggled to define its identity and relevance within the broader media company. The CEO of the dot.com subsidiary was addressing the challenges of being an executive of a small subsidiary to a much larger formal conglomerate. The cultures were complete opposites. However, as a subsidiary of a privately owned, conservative conglomerate, they weren't considered executives on the company's leadership team.*

In the simplest terms, executives develop and execute a company's short- and long-term strategies. If a person can materially impact performance or results, or have P&L responsibility, and has a position with significant responsibility and/

or complexity, he or she is an executive. As a result, these roles are single-incumbent positions (in other words, there is only one person in that role with that title—there's *one* CFO, *one* controller, and *one* HR manager, as opposed to three accounts payable clerks). The people in these roles may lead departments and/or critical strategies. They may or may not directly supervise other employees. They may or may not be the most significantly compensated employees within the firm. And, as I learned throughout the course of my career, executives don't only wear three-piece suits. Furthermore, significant compensation levels or wealth accumulation does not make a person an executive. Just lucky.

I have partnered with start-up firms whose executives worked in a warehouse separated by cubicles and meeting rooms—not offices. As the company grew, the number of cubes increased, but the executives still enjoyed cubicles, wore jeans, and brought their pets to work. At another firm that went public prior to our engagement, the company maintained its startup culture with a concierge, basketball court, and cafeteria. This company was led by seasoned executives from mature organizations, brought in to propel the company forward. They stood out, until they finally exchanged their ties and blazers for button-down shirts and khakis.

Whereas some industries are male-dominated (for example, financial services and entertainment), others boast a significant female presence in the executive ranks (for example, in advertising, marketing, fashion, and healthcare). One client I worked with, a fashion house, had the same high-performing, high-stress, and high-pressure environment of any NYC investment firm. The executives there—predominantly women—preferred female consultants. When I participated in meetings at this fashion house, I felt in awe of these women—their stature, intelligence, and accomplishments.

At the opposite end of the spectrum, I once partnered with a not-for-profit organization housed in a less-than-desirable area of a city. We scheduled all meetings during daylight hours and dressed down. Way down. These executives, dressed in jeans and sneakers, pursued a noble mission helping disadvantaged youth in their area.

> Not-for-profits maintain competitive compensation, similar to for-profits. However, their "executive" compensation programs must comply with the Intermediate Sanctions Section 4958 stipulation that all compensation and benefits provided to disqualified persons in a nonprofit must be reasonable. In a not-for-profit, a "disqualified person" is considered an executive. These individuals must have strategic impact over the finances or decision-making of the organization, but can also be a child of someone with this influence. More importantly, their pay must be "reasonable" (not competitive, but reasonable). In order to fulfill these IRS requirements and maintain their not-for-profit status, not-for-profit organizations engage in extremely rigorous annual reviews to ensure transparency and accountability.

Whether public or private, for-profit or not-for-profit, the executive pool must first be defined. Only after determining which positions qualify as "executives" within a company or organization can the compensation programs be identified and reviewed.

The main difference, from a compensation perspective, between executives and the broader employee population is the types of programs offered—not just the level of compensation. In other words, executive compensation comprises the awards (both compensation *and* benefits) allocated to executives within an individual firm or organization. The purpose of executive compensation is threefold:

1. Attract and retain the right talent.

2. Motivate behaviors and decision-making in a manner that achieves a company's short- and long-term business strategies.

3. Reward outcomes appropriately, based on performance, and ensure alignment of programs with stakeholder/shareholder interests.

So what does a "good" compensation program look like? What do you think of when you think of "compensation"? Base? Bonus? What about retirement? Do you think your program is competitive? How do you know?

The Compensation Philosophy

A comprehensive compensation program is governed by a well-articulated (Board or management approved) compensation philosophy. Companies then employ mechanisms and tools such as base salary and long-term incentives to achieve their desired compensation philosophy.

*During a meeting with a female HR executive, she explained their philosophy: Provide everything at the 75th percentile. And she meant **everything**—pay, health and welfare benefits, retirement, and perquisites. She must have sensed my hesitation because she continued to explain, "No one wants to work for this company. We can't even have our logo showing on our stuff." She told me the story of someone who was given a travel coffee mug with the logo. This person, although grateful, was seen tossing it in the garbage because he did not want to publicize the fact that he worked for that company.*

The compensation philosophy becomes the guiding principle—the roadmap—for how pay is delivered. A compensation philosophy includes elements such as industry, market targets, peers, company size, and business objectives. A well-designed compensation philosophy will articulate who the company compares itself to (its peers) when gathering competitive market data. The competitive market data is then used to analyze its pay program.

A compensation philosophy serves the following corporate objectives:

1. Identify the organization's pay programs and total reward vehicles to be utilized.

2. Identify how the pay programs and strategies will support the company's business strategy, competitive outlook, operating objectives, and human capital needs.

3. Attract, retain, and motivate employees.

4. Define the competitive market position the company will target with regard to base pay, variable compensation (annual and long-term incentives), and benefits (health and welfare, and retirement).

A company determines (and measures) how it rewards its employees using this compensation philosophy. Should base salary be targeted at market median (50th percentile), or below market? Should annual incentives provide total cash compensation (base plus bonus) levels at or above the 75th percentile? Or should base salary target below the market 50th percentile, with annual incentives comprising a larger portion of total cash compensation in order to achieve a 75th percentile total cash (base plus bonus) positioning? Will long-term incentives be utilized? How? How does that support the philosophy? And what about benefits? Will robust benefits be used to compensate for less competitive cash compensation? These are all questions companies consider when developing their compensation philosophy.

A company with limited cash flow may opt to use equity as its main reward mechanism. Private companies with no external market for liquidating equity may reward employees with cash compensation, "phantom" long-term incentives (such as units or shares), and benefits. The current growth stage of the company and its financial solvency will greatly impact its compensation philosophy.

Public companies document their compensation philosophies, as required by the SEC, in public proxy filings. Martha Stewart Omnimedia's 2013 proxy detailed the following philosophy:

Our compensation philosophy is guided by our belief that achievement of our business goals depends on attracting and retaining executives with an appropriate combination of creative skill and managerial expertise. Our compensation program is designed to attract such executives and align their total compensation with the short- and long-term performance of the Company. The Company's compensation program is composed of base salary, annual bonus, and equity compensation.

We provide our senior executives with base salaries commensurate with their backgrounds, skill sets, and responsibilities;

We provide the opportunity to earn annual bonuses that are intended to reward our executives based on the performance of our Company and that of the executive; and

We make equity awards that vest over time in order to induce executives to remain in our employ and to align their interests with those of our other stockholders.

We have moved towards equity compensation packages based primarily on stock options and RSUs because we believe these longer-term awards better align our executives' interests with those of other stockholders.

Learning Your Company's Compensation Philosophy

The first step in playing the money game and winning is to learn *your* company's compensation philosophy. As I mentioned with the Martha Stewart example, public companies must articulate their executive compensation philosophy in their publicly filed proxy (DEF14A) statement. Privately held companies may communicate their compensation philosophies on their intranet or in internally produced documents. If neither resource is available, ask your manager.

The compensation philosophy used for the broad-based population of employees will mirror the compensation philosophy used for executives, minus the use of various rewards vehicles. Companies will not pay their executives at the 75th percentile of base pay and everyone else at the 25th percentile; the compensation philosophy trickles down through the organization. (However, there is one caveat: special roles such as sales positions that are highly leveraged or commission-based will have a different philosophy.)

Here's another example of a compensation philosophy, this one from Nike (from its proxy filed July 27, 2012):

> *"...our executive compensation program is aligned with our business strategy and culture to attract and retain top talent, reward business results and individual performance, and, most importantly, maximize shareholder returns. Our total compensation program for the Named Executive Officers is highly incentive-based and competitive in the marketplace, with Company performance determining a significant portion of total compensation. Our program consists of the following elements:*
>
> **ɸ** *Base salary that reflects the executive's accountabilities, skills, experience, performance, and future potential*
>
> **ɸ** *Annual performance-based incentive cash bonus based on Company financial results under our Executive Performance Sharing Plan*

❍ *A portfolio approach to long-term incentive compensation to provide a balanced mix of equity and performance-based cash incentives, including:*

    ❍ *Performance-based cash awards based on Company financial results under the Long-Term Incentive Plan to encourage attainment of long-term financial objectives*

    ❍ *Stock options to align the interests of executives with those of shareholders*

    ❍ *Restricted stock awards and restricted stock unit retention awards to provide incentives consistent with shareholder returns, and to provide strong retention incentives*

    ❍ *Benefits*

    ❍ *Profit sharing contributions to defined contribution retirement plans*

    ❍ *Post-termination payments under non-competition or employment agreements*

Defining Peer Groups

When developing a compensation philosophy, identifying whom to include in a peer group becomes critical. A company considers both its business objectives and the market for talent (which comprises the market for business and the market for labor). The two may not be symbiotic. Why do peers matter? Well, for example, a company that competes in the electronic hardware supplier space will consider its specific competitors for business—where do its customers source bids, products, and services? These are its competitors for business. Its competitors for talent, however, may represent a broader swathe. Certain positions, such as human resources or finance, span industries because their skillsets are transferable. Therefore, these positions may include market data based on competitors for business *and* competitors for talent. How the data is mixed and used is determined by the compensation philosophy. A heavier weight may be placed on business industry peers, or the data may be weighted equally. Additionally, peer groups may be different by level, as well as function. Division, or subsidiary executives can face different peer groups, depending on the business's diversity and the parent company's philosophy and approach to compensation.

> *One client struggled immensely with its peer group discussion after it went public and achieved significant levels of growth and stock price appreciation. Its peers morphed from being private companies to being public companies with numerous divisions, products, and assets with shorter or longer useful lives. These public companies were significantly larger in terms of revenue and maturity. This company questioned the appropriateness of including them in the peer group and possibly inflating compensation levels.*

Defining the appropriate peer group requires intense discussion, deliberation, and agreement.

8 Common Compensation Elements

Once a compensation philosophy is developed and approved, companies implement individual pay vehicles to achieve their philosophy. Think of it as pieces of a puzzle. Although many of these vehicles can, and are used for all employees, the following items are commonly included to deliver a comprehensive *executive* compensation program. Each element serves the purpose of attracting, retaining, and motivating executive-level employees, as well as minimizing risk and liability.

1. Base salary
2. Annual incentives (bonus)
3. Long-term incentives
4. Severance plans
5. Change-in-control agreements/policy
6. (Supplemental) nonqualified health and welfare benefits
7. (Supplemental) nonqualified retirement plans
8. Perquisites

In the following pages I'll describe each of the eight components and, more importantly, how companies use them. This information—more detailed and less thrilling than most conversations—conveys what you could be expecting as your career progresses. I provide the definition and intent of each vehicle, but not the competitive level you could be expecting because competitiveness varies by role, industry, and company size.

Remember, knowledge is power. Knowing what you can, could, or should be asking for significantly improves your negotiating position.

1. Base Salary

Definition: The fixed, recurring part of total compensation. It is what employees receive for performing their duties and responsibilities.

Intention: To attract the right individuals to perform the duties and responsibilities of a particular role in a satisfactory manner.

2. Annual Incentives (Bonus)

Definition: The additional (or incremental) amount received for achieving goals within a 12-month (or shorter) time frame. Annual incentives can be delivered in cash and/or equity.

Intention: To tie individual performance to the achievement of specific, measurable, short-term company objectives. Companies also use incentives as a means of placing a greater portion of total cash compensation "at risk," which means these incentives are not guaranteed, and also for managing expenses. Incentives typically do not pay out unless specific financial measures are achieved. Once the company wins, by achieving additional revenue or profit, the plan pays out.

> **Note:** *Sales roles typically use commission-based plans. Commissions fall in the short-term incentive bucket, but the time period can be monthly or quarterly. These plans are typically highly leveraged: low base (for example, $25k) relative to a higher bonus (for example, $75k) as a percent of base.*

The combination of base salary and annual incentives (or bonuses) is commonly referred to as *total cash compensation.* The particular mix of the two, called the "leverage," varies depending on the company, the industry, and the company's compensation philosophy. Here's an example: Person A earns $100k annually. Person B also earns $100k annually. Person A has a base salary of $80k and an *actual* bonus (this is the bonus received—not necessarily the maximum amount Person A could have earned) of $20k, or 20 percent. Person B has a base salary of $25k and bonus of $75k. Person B's package is highly leveraged—only a small portion is fixed (guaranteed). Why would Person B want this type of pay package? Person B might be in sales. Sales individuals are compensated with highly leveraged packages to motivate them to build the business, expand accounts, and secure new business. Person B might even have the potential to earn $200k annually, depending on performance. This example shows how two packages may seem similar on the surface but can actually be quite different and intended for different purposes.

3. Long-Term Incentives

Definition: The additional (or incremental) amount earned for achieving goals aligned with a timeframe longer than one year (typically three to five years). Long-term incentives can be delivered in cash, equity, or units. The most common long-term incentives are non-qualified stock options and restricted stock.

"Stock options" are a *right* to *purchase* stock in the future (after a vesting schedule), whereas "restricted stock" has value currently (the actual share is granted) but cannot be accessed until after it has vested. The value of stock options will be the difference between the value at grant and the value at exercise (minus taxes). Stock options sometimes cause confusion because, although they have an "expected value," the actual value at the date of grant is zero. The stock price needs to increase for the stock to have value. "Vesting" refers to the conveying or transference of ownership. Vesting can be time-based (for example, a third of the total grant may "vest" per year) or performance-based (grant recipients may have ownership of a third of the grant after a performance measure is achieved). The value of restricted stock will be the difference between the value at grant and the value at exercise (minus taxes), although the strike price (the grant price or fair market value of the stock price on the day it is granted to the employee) is typically $0. In other words, restricted stock is generally worth the total price (fair market value) at grant.

The combination of cash compensation and long-term incentives is referred to as *total direct compensation.*

Intention: To ensure individuals develop and implement decisions that support long-term business strategies. From a compensation perspective, equity long-term incentives can be used to alleviate the pressure on cash as the only vehicle for delivering compensation.

Remember, if you receive options, the stock price needs to increase above the grant price in order for the options to have value. Plus there are tax implications: You will be taxed upon vesting. You can exercise options upon vesting to cover the taxes, but it is important to consider these factors when determining their value in your total compensation package.

The following chart illustrates a couple of stock option scenarios to help you understand how it works in terms of compensation.

Stock Price	# of shares granted	Vesting Schedule (the rate at which you can ACCESS the options or EXERCISE them)	When long-term incentive is exercisable (when options/ shares vest)	Value
$20	10,000 (stock options)	¼ per year	$25	**IN THE MONEY.** Each VESTED option (2,500 after year 1) is worth $5 per share (minus taxes).
$20	10,000 (stock options)	¼ per year	$15	**UNDERWATER.** The shares are not worth anything because the stock price is less than the grant price.
$0	10,000 restricted shares	¼ per year	$20	**IN THE MONEY.** Each share (2,500 after year 1) is worth $20 (minus taxes).

4. Severance

Definition: Payments made to individuals who are terminated *without cause*. Severance can be paid in one lump sum or monthly, and can consist of base salary only or base, bonus, and benefits. Severance can also be paid to individuals terminated *with* cause, in exchange for a respectful and speedy separation from the company.

Intention: To ensure individuals continue to act in the company's best interests, regardless of the potential impact to their employment. Severance policies protect companies by ensuring that employees execute the right business decisions—regardless of whether the decisions result in job loss.

To effectively grow businesses, companies need to implement strategies that benefit the company, brand, shareholders/stakeholders, and key investors. Companies institute severance policies to ensure that individuals act in good faith, regardless of the possible employment outcomes. By protecting individuals financially, companies ensure an individual will execute proper decisions, regardless of employment. For example, if a proper severance package is in place, an individual will negotiate a divestiture to the best of his or her ability, recognizing that his or her job may be in jeopardy (terminated, eliminated, or divested with the company).

At the executive level, severance amounts are not based on tenure but on level. These positions tend to turn over more frequently and it takes longer for these individuals to find comparable jobs that earn the same level of income.

5. Change-in-Control Agreements/Policy

Definition: An element included in the plan documents for various compensation vehicles such as long-term incentives or deferred compensation that protects individuals' earnings under a change-in-control (CIC) scenario. The plan document will define a CIC, typically including a change in ownership by more than 50 percent. Under a CIC, equity may vest immediately.

Intention: Similar to severance policies, CIC provisions ensure individuals act in the company's best interests because their compensation is protected. For example, a merger typically triggers a CIC. Unvested equity may vest upon a double trigger—change-in-control and termination without cause—and allow the individual to access his or her equity immediately.

6. (Supplemental) Nonqualified Health and Welfare Benefits

Definition: Health and welfare (in other words, medical) benefits that are *only* awarded to executives, and therefore are considered nonqualified, as opposed to qualified benefits, which are available to all employees. Companies also provide the option for supplemental benefits such as supplemental life insurance or supplemental disability that can be purchased by an employee.

Intention: To provide full coverage to executives, in line with their salary and level within the company.

For example, a company may provide an executive with a supplemental long-term disability (LTD) plan. If the current LTD plan provides a payout equal to two times salary, with a maximum of $500,000, then individuals earning more than $250,000 will not receive the *intended* benefit. Therefore, a company may secure an additional policy (supplemental benefit) in order to provide this person with two times the salary. Alternatively, the qualified long-term plan may only cover salary and have a cap. The plan may not cover the other portion of an executive's income, such as incentives or retirement savings. This can be covered by a supplemental plan.

7. (Supplemental) Nonqualified Retirement Plans

Definition: Companies typically offer qualified plans to individuals to allow them to defer a portion of their earnings until retirement. An example of this is the 401(k). The yearly maximum allowable 401(k) contribution as determined by the Internal Revenue Code in 2013 was $17,500. Supplemental executive retirement plans (SERPs), on the other hand, are *nonqualified*. In this case money is withdrawn into an investment account, thereby reducing current income taxes. Additionally, potential investment earnings won't be taxable until withdrawn at retirement. If employers offer a supplemental retirement plan, they determine the investment choices and other plan features. Then participants decide how much to contribute and to which investments.

Intention: Supplemental retirement plans provide tax-deferred savings to allow executives to defer additional income for retirement beyond the basic retirement plan their employer offers. A SERP allows a company to provide the *intended* benefit. For example, if someone earns $50,000 a year and contributes the maximum $17,000, he is deferring 34 percent of his annual income. Conversely, if an executive earns $200,000 and contributes the maximum $17,000, she is only deferring 8.5 percent of her income. Because of the executive's higher income, she is unable to defer a comparable amount. The SERP compensates for this difference.

As another example, some companies provide deferred compensation arrangements, whereby plan participants can voluntarily defer a portion of their base salary and/or annual incentive until several years later (typically at least five or until retirement). The money is placed in a trust which is then managed like a fund. To encourage individuals to participate, companies may offer to match a percentage of the deferred income (in other words, provide additional income).

8. Perquisites

Definition: Additional items provided to individuals outside of their compensation and benefits. Examples of perquisites include a company car, car allowance, usage of a company jet/airplane, and automatic upgrade to business or first-class airline seats.

Intention: Companies employ these "perks" to facilitate executive performance or further define their role and level within an organization.

A Note about the Media

The media report publicly available pay disclosures during times of depressed stock prices, scandal, or whenever the pay seems outrageous. It is important to note that journalists only copy what is filed by the company with the SEC. They do not analyze, understand, or interpret the figures. The resulting media frenzy promotes sales, clicks, followers, and tweets, but not necessarily the truth.

In January 2013, when Marissa Mayer first took the helm of Yahoo!, news outlets reported on her seemingly "excessive" compensation. The internet devoured her potential $100 million in compensation. Out of context, $100 million seems ludicrous. The article further details that Ms. Mayer is expected to receive around $5.4 million from Yahoo! for 2013 and around $20 million a year after that, though some of that amount is tied to performance targets set by the board.

Off the cuff, the package seems exorbitant. The article, unfortunately, continues to compare her pay to her predecessors' compensation. Ms. Mayer's predecessors, Scott Thompson and Carol Bartz, received compensation packages worth $27 million and $44.6 million, respectively, over several years. Furthermore, both CEOs departed prematurely. Mr. Thompson resigned in May after a five-month stint, whereas Ms. Bartz was fired after two and a half years at Yahoo!.

This is where the media get it wrong. They only report numbers, without any education, background, or context. First, precedence has only some bearing on compensation provided to future CEOs. What matters is what is happening *now*. Additionally, Mayer's package included a buy-out. In other words, Mayer had options with value at her previous employer, Google, that she had not exercised, and Yahoo! was partially compensating her (approximately $14 million) for those options because she essentially walked away from the payout to join Yahoo!. This is common practice—not just for CEOs but anyone leaving "in-the-money" options on the table.

She was also being paid a one-time retention award of $15 million that vests over five years (or $3 million per year). Based on how the last two CEOs were publicly and unceremoniously dumped, a retention award seems reasonable. No high-performing person would take that job without substantial compensation. The risk is too high. For comparison purposes the $3 million per year ($15 million total) should not be included when comparing her compensation to other CEOs.

As a result, Mayer is probably receiving a base, bonus, and equity grant worth approximately $70 million. *But not $70 million each year.* The full details would have been disclosed in Yahoo!'s next proxy, which had yet to be filed at the time the *WSJ* article was published. The *WSJ* gleaned their information from an equity regulatory filing that does not detail Mayer's full package or provide any explanation.

My point? Don't let the media mislead you.

Conclusion

Ostensibly, companies want to reward employees competitively for their efforts—hence the term pay-for-performance. Therefore, most companies create reasonable, competitive, transparent, and accountable total rewards (compensation and benefit) programs that both support and promote its business strategies to ensure each employee and stakeholder reaps the benefits.

CHAPTER 2

The Role of the Consultant

"I do not want to create a program
that will rob Peter to pay Paul."
—Senior executive of a global Fortune 500 company

And neither did I. Contrary to what the mainstream media would have you believe, executive compensation consultants do not arbitrarily establish pay levels. Companies and their consultants work together to ensure that compensation programs attract, retain, and motivate high performers as well as align individual behaviors with the company's short- and long-term business strategies. The process is data-driven, analytical, and methodical, and develops a strong foundation for robust decision-making. The ultimate objectives—transparency, accountability, and objectivity—are shared mutually by all parties.

Compensation consulting as an industry is relatively new. Only a few practices (generally subsidiaries of larger firms) existed in the early 1960s and 1970s. Firms such as McKinsey, Bain, and Towers Watson leveraged small, profitable compensation consulting practices that received recognition and gained momentum in both growth and prestige. In the 1980s, when executive pay began to increase more rapidly (and become a regular part of mainstream conversations), the once small compensation consulting industry expanded exponentially.

Do a Google search for "executive compensation consulting" and at least 10 pages of unique consulting firms will appear. And, because both management and Boards of Directors can (and do) hire their own consultants, the number of mainstream and boutique firms specializing in executive compensation has catapulted. The cream of the crop (like Towers) now competes with global, regional, and boutique firms.

Industry-recognized Fortune 100 Board-level consultants impart advice, guide Board member decision-making, and resolve critical issues. One such man, Fred Cook, made a name for himself as a top executive compensation advisor. Cook, a veritable God in the executive compensation world, began his career with Towers Perrin in 1966. In 1973, at age 32, he launched the firm that bears his name: Frederic W. Cook & Co. During his years with Towers Perrin, few corporate boards even had compensation committees. In 1988, Cook devised the ingenious and widely used "reload option," which planted him and his company firmly on the map. Think of the reload option like a Starbucks reward card: You can get new options after you exercise, or use, the original options. At a very high level, it's like getting five new lattes after you drank the five you were originally gifted. Since then, Cook's firm has advised more than 1,800 clients and at least half of the Fortune 500.

In 1996, being an executive compensation consultant garnered respect. And retaining a prestigious firm, with highly regarded compensation experts, added credibility to the decision-making process and gave comfort to the shareholders.

One of my first client engagements focused on reviewing the executive compensation practices and programs for a global company. The head of human resources—female—reported to a "no-nonsense" CEO. She hired us to add credibility and authority to the process because both management and the Board of Directors demanded external expertise and accountability. She also hired us to "manage" the politics. In essence, the head of human resources understood that if the recommendations came solely from her—without external validation—their chances of being approved diminished greatly.

After a few years of interacting with senior executives and Board members at various firms in a variety of industries, I ascertained three more important life lessons:

My fifth real life lesson: *Reputation trumps greed (for most people).* Executives care deeply about their own compensation, but they do not want to be pummeled on the front page of the *New York Times* or *Wall Street Journal*.

My sixth real life lesson: *Most companies recognize the value of executive compensation advice.* Companies partner with

external consultants to review and recommend the strategy
and processes for their pay programs to ensure:

- internal and external competitiveness
- a strong linkage to both the short- and long-term
  business strategies
- transparency
- accountability
- responsible behaviors

My seventh real life lesson: *Companies will* always *value
executive compensation advice.* Companies invest in determining the accuracy and reasonableness of their executive compensation programs because of their constantly changing business needs and economic drivers, and because executives either
drive successes or limit failures.

Without a doubt, it is an interesting profession. Government
regulation, public perception, and economic climate changes
necessitate constantly evaluating and re-evaluating programs.
Issues surface, causing programs to be constantly monitored,
and therefore clients abound. Yet, ten years after I started, the
profession that once seemed respectful became shrouded in
controversy and suspicion. In 2002, images of shredded documents and Enron-related implosions changed how the public
perceived and even understood executive compensation. Water-
cooler talk suggested executive compensation consultants con-
tributed to the financial services industry implosion in 2006.
Supposedly inflated pay levels and allegedly mismanaged incentives caused improper decision-making, Ponzi schemes, and
an overall house of cards. People linked executive compensation with using the company jet for personal travel or purchas-
ing $14,000 shower curtains (à la Quest).

Discussing my profession caused stress—I had to explain the process in detail, defend the ethics and morality, and re-affirm that not all executives are dirty rotten scoundrels. In fact, most compensation consulting firms are honest, hard-working, highly ethical companies that strive to provide value for shareholders while paying the people that deliver this value competitively.

Today, executive compensation consultants need to be as transparent as the executives themselves. Public companies must disclose who they retain as consultants and how much they pay them. Stakeholders, the media, and government regulators demand independence, transparency, and accountability from executive compensation consultants. In June 2012, the Securities and Exchange Commission (SEC) approved a new rule from the Dodd-Frank Wall Street Reform and Consumer Protection Act, requiring exchange listing companies to address:

- The Board of Directors' compensation committee member independence
- The Board compensation committee's authority to hire compensation consultants
- The committee's review of the adviser's independence
- The committee's responsibility for overseeing the work of any compensation consultants

The rule "encourages" Boards to act independently (as though they already aren't) from management as well as to fulfill their fiduciary duties. The financial services industry implosion highlighted the importance of executive compensation consultant independence. Federal regulators feared executive compensation consultants' objectivity was impaired if the same firm also provided benefit/actuarial services to the consulting company. Annual benefit/actuarial services can result in millions of dollars in annual revenues for the consulting firm, and politicians feared executive compensation consultants were padding pay levels to ensure their firms retained the benefit/actuarial work.

And yet, in all my years providing executive compensation consulting advice, this was *never* an issue.

Never.

But from an "optics" perspective, perception = reality, so independence remains critical. Therefore companies began to divide the work among various firms rather than award one firm both the executive compensation and benefits services. The SEC recommends that consulting firms take into account the fees received and any potential conflicts of interest, but it does not expressly prohibit companies from retaining the same firm to conduct both executive and benefit/actuarial services.

Start-ups, pre-IPOs, early stage private firms, and nonprofits act just as vigilantly, protecting their reputation and brand. Tarnished images (think of Lance Armstrong's impact on Livestrong) seriously impede revenue, growth, and funding. I have worked with billion-dollar not-for-profits to ensure their pay programs remained competitive yet defensible, especially in light of public scrutiny. In many ways, these organizations are subject to a higher level of scrutiny than public firms because of their missions and brand.

In my extensive experience, the role of the consultant should include:

- ◑ Being up to date on government regulation, industry practices, and accounting tax implications

● Developing programs that link compensation payouts to company performance—payouts that trickle down throughout the organization

● Acting as a trusted advisor

● Providing reasonable recommendations

● Walking away, if necessary

> *I once worked with an organization where the CEO was receiving compensation that required further alignment with the organization's goals. After exploring the issues, I learned that the company was unwilling to make the alignments necessary to ensure good governance. The HR manager (one of the few women in the office) had little to no influence. Our team ended up walking away.*

The Executive Compensation Process

Regardless of whether executive pay rates are water-cooler gossip, front-page news, or proxy-disclosed information, individuals who participate in—and understand—the full process can better leverage the available information to maximize their compensation opportunities.

Understanding the process—and how *your* role impacts (or is part of) the process—is critical to maximizing compensation and earning competitive pay levels, comparable with your peers and your performance.

So now let's talk about the process.

The remainder of this chapter details the steps involved in the executive compensation process, and how executives can (and should) be involved. I focus on the executive compensation process because it is comprehensive (in terms of all the compensation elements that could be reviewed/included), thorough (because it involves all the players), and illustrates the extent of individual involvement. The process consultants follow to develop broadbased compensation programs closely mirrors this discussion.

To conduct a thorough competitive executive compensation review, several critical steps are involved:

1. The company sends out requests for proposal (RFPs).

2. Consultants detail their proposed work via three phases:

   a. Discovery phase

   b. Assessment/analysis phase

   c. Recommendations phase

1. The Company Sends out Requests for Proposal (RFPs)

Companies select compensation consultants because they do not currently retain consultants, because they want to change consultants, or because they want to reconfirm the fees and services the current consultants provide. They do this by developing an RFP (request for proposal). A company's RFP includes the scope of the work needed, the company's desired outcomes and timeframe, and contractual obligations. Potential consultants review the scope, clarify questions with the company, and develop a proposal.

Companies then interview consultants, compare proposals, and select the consultants that best meet their needs. Some organizations employ purchasing/procurement departments or outside procurement firms to secure proposals from firms. The theory behind using procurement firms is that it's more efficient and establishes an objective and fair selection process.

> *Most public sector employers (government agencies) select consultants using a prescribed procurement process. I attended question and answer sessions for many federal and local government agency RFP's. These sessions— administered by the procurement department— are highly formal and regimented. Working both with and at a public sector organization requires details and precisions—and the patience to work within a highly bureaucratic culture.*

2. The Consultants Propose Work

Consultants employ a variety of methods to conduct compensation reviews/assessments and develop recommendations. Generally, the process involves the combination of three perspectives: external benchmarking, internal reviews, and overall program design expertise. A comprehensive process comprises a discovery phase, an assessment/analysis phase, and a recommendation phase. Depending on the agreed-upon outcomes, an additional phase (design or re-design) may be included.

Phase 1: Discovery

In most situations, interviewing key executives and Board members proves extremely desirable, informative, and necessary for successful project outcomes. The interview process unearths the Board's understanding of both short- and long-term business strategies, the compensation program, and how the compensation program is (and should be) used to reward performance. Almost always, discrepancies arise. Sometimes Board members or some executives believe one or two strategic items are imperative while other individuals focus on other initiatives. To develop a successful compensation program, everyone needs to be on the same page. Including interviews in the process guarantees a more successful outcome because the differences can be ironed out up front. Because the interviews are confidential, consultants gain an excellent view of Board members' personalities, business agendas, cultural perceptions, and beliefs.

In addition to conducting interviews, consultants scour, research, and review compensation and human resources plan documents and strategic plans. In essence, consultants absorb as much information as possible about the company's strategy and programs during the discovery phase. Key questions are addressed, such as: Why is this review desired? Is there a new CEO? New management team? Does the company need to add key individuals to its management team? Is the company planning on divesting any businesses? Where does the company hire its executive talent? With whom does the company compete for business? What are the short-term business objectives? Long-term? How has the industry been performing? How does the company perform against the industry? What is the company's growth strategy? What compensation (and benefits) programs are currently being offered? The questions are endless and vary enormously depending on the situation.

Phase 2: Assessment/Analysis

First, the stake gets put in the ground. What has the company been doing in terms of compensation? What is the value of its current compensation levels (by incumbent or role)? What are the market values of benchmark jobs? How do the current market values compare to the company's current philosophy?

To conduct this market assessment, jobs must be matched to survey data roles, and the corresponding market data must be compiled. To determine which market data to gather, the consultants need to know who the company should be compared against. For example, if a $3 billion medical devices firm is comparing its Head of Brand Marketing to other Heads of Brand Marketing within its industry at comparably sized organizations, (a) the role needs to be matched to the appropriate brand executive (titles alone are insufficient; job descriptions must be used), and (b) the data listed for companies with similar revenues must be gathered.

Therefore, one critical action needs to occur: peer group identification.

The peer group comprises the company's business and talent competitors. These are not necessarily one and the same. The larger and the more stable the peer group (companies do not drop in and out each year; the group itself stays relatively constant), the greater the data's validity. The Board of Directors typically approves the peer group. Without an approved peer group, the data can be questioned in terms of reliability and appropriateness. For example, if the medical devices firmed compared its compensation for the Head of Brand Marketing role only to advertising or other agency firms, the data could be considered flawed.

> *Companies typically establish a peer group with the intention of maintaining it for at least three years—for consistency and comparability. For comparison purposes, one peer is never swapped out for another peer. At least two peers much change to ensure the data remains statistically valid.*

Second, to determine which market data should be compared to which incumbent roles and compensation, the roles must be appropriately matched to survey job descriptions. This step is critical because titles do not accurately reflect responsibilities; a job title employed at one corporation may comprise different duties than the same title at another corporation. Consultants use two primary tactics when matching roles: job descriptions and interview discussions. Both approaches unveil a job's roles and responsibilities. Note that the focus is on the *primary* roles and responsibilities. If, for example, an individual spends less than 10 percent of his/her time doing a certain task, that task may not be considered relevant and therefore will not impact the job match.

This is an important part of the process. In my experience, men are more likely to capitalize on the opportunity to interview with consultants to detail *everything* they do—and the importance of everything they do. On the other hand, women use the opportunity to explain only the bulk of their job. Women are more like to impart the info they think consultants need to accurately price their job whereas men generally never assume what consultants need to know. Men rarely assume what is important and what isn't important; women are much more likely to do so. Whichever gender you are, if you have the opportunity to be interviewed, do provide the interviewer with information on *everything* you do, and stress the *importance* of everything you do. Even if one part of your job takes 10 percent of your time, do not assume it has 10 percent importance. Its importance might be critical to the future direction of the company. The consultant will synthesize the information to determine the right benchmark.

Third, once the Board approves the peer group (not just management), data can then be gathered and analyzed from these peers. Consulting firms collect market data (using the pre-approved peer group) using custom surveys (selected companies and specialized roles) or published (industry-wide with common roles) compensation surveys. Furthermore, the firms that develop this data "clean" the data. Jobs are matched based on responsibilities rather than title, and the compensation is analyzed and questioned rather than just accepted carte blanche.

If you have ever perused Websites to check "market rates," keep in mind they do not "clean" the data. The Websites do not confirm that either the matches used or the data supplied is appropriate or correct. This data should be taken with a grain of salt.

Data is gathered and independently arrayed, and statistics are generated for each role. Surveys generate statistically valid market data for each role at the 25th, 50th, or 75th percentiles. Using a published (or custom) compensation survey also adds credibility and accountability. Statistically, the data is valid and the process can be repeated year after year. When conducting analyses, consultants compare the company's current compensation offered to the peer group's 25th, 50th, and 75th percentile data. The company generally targets a desired market percentile for each compensation element as part of its compensation philosophy.

Market Analysis Illustration

In the first chapter, I conveyed Martha Stewart Omnimedia's compensation philosophy. Using that company, the following table illustratively compares the CEO's base salary levels to fictitious market data.

Incumbent	Current Base Salary	Market Base Salary			% Difference		
		25th	50th	75th	25th	50th	75th
Charles Koppleman	$990k	$925k	$975k	$1,250k	7.0%	1.5%	-20.8%

Remember that this is not an exact science (remember the Introduction: it's objective *and* subjective). These data points are just that—reference points. Additionally, a range of reasonableness is considered competitive. Using the fictitious example I just gave, knowing Martha Stewart Omnimedia targets the 50th percentile for base salary, Mr. Koppleman's current base salary levels seem competitive because his pay exceeds the 50th percentile by only 1.5 percent. If the company targeted the 75th percentile, his base salary may appear to be lagging.

Fourth, the process further compares both actual and target compensation levels. Actual compensation is what the company delivered. Target compensation levels are what the company *intended* to deliver if predetermined performance objectives were met. Actual pay may be substantially different from target pay depending on the individual and the financial performance he/she achieved. Analyzing actual pay and target pay help determine whether the plan itself (the target payout levels) are competitive. Actual pay can fall significantly below market (assuming performance objectives were not achieved), but as long as target pay dances within competitive levels, the program is considered competitive.

Consultants examine the following elements of compensation:

- Actual total cash compensation = base salary plus actual annual incentives received
- Target total cash compensation = base salary plus the target annual incentive
- Actual total direct compensation = actual total cash compensation plus the expected value of long-term incentives (such as stock options) delivered
- Target total direct compensation = target total cash compensation plus the value of long-term incentives (such as stock options) delivered

Again, the purpose of evaluating both actual and target levels is to confirm the competitiveness and reasonableness of the plan design.

Phase 3: Recommendations

In light of the data analyzed, combined with the company's business strategy and compensation philosophy, consultants determine whether the current program supports current and desired strategic objectives. Measures, eligibility, and performance levels receive critical attention. Are individuals being paid for achieving the right levels of financial performance? Are the right financial measures being employed? Are the financial measures used in the incentive plans supporting the company's strategies and desired decision-making?

Using the data (both quantitative and qualitative) gathered and analyzed, consultants may recommend that programs be redesigned, added, or eliminated. Business practices, culture, and cost constraints fuel recommendations as well. Here are a few examples of this:

- Results may indicate that the majority of individuals receive pay levels significantly below market. Substantial increases to competitive pay levels not only increases compensation but benefit expenses as well, so companies may adjust base salary levels over time rather than all at once.

- Implementing a formalized annual incentive plan may be paramount. However, to have a successful annual incentive plan, companies must engage in robust performance management processes. A company may be able to design the right incentive plan but not have the human capital resources or the technology to effectively implement a performance management program necessary for managing the annual incentive plan. This may occur in stages or require simplifying the plan or developing more comprehensive employee communication.

- Mature companies that grant annual stock options to all employees may no longer have the available equity to continue this practice. Grant levels and/or eligibility may be severely reduced. Companies may replace equity grants with other rewards or eliminate grants as part of the overall remuneration. Significant employee communications must be engaged to transition employee perceptions and commitment under the new arrangement.

I once worked with a global company, headquartered in the Washington, D.C. area, whose human resources department wanted to integrate a formal annual incentive program. Because the agency is global, a formal program would be countercultural in many countries. Therefore a discretionary plan was implemented until the organization could be culturally transitioned to using a more formalized plan that included predetermined objectives and measures.

Understanding the process and its components is critical for maximizing compensation. After discussing the four most common female personality powerhouses in Chapter 4, I will revisit this process and discuss how women can leverage their personalities and knowledge of the compensation process to maximize their earnings.

Regarding Not-for-Profits

Not-for-profit organizations—specifically 501(c)(3) and 501(c)(4) tax-exempt employers—must comply with section 4958 of the Internal Revenue code to avoid Intermediate Sanctions regulations. In essence, Intermediate Sanctions are interest and excise penalties that can be imposed on any disqualified person (and any organization manager who approved the benefit) deemed to have received an "excess benefit," or unreasonable compensation, from the organization. However, Congress created a rebuttable presumption of *reasonableness*, or safe harbor—like the "Get out of Jail Free" card in Monopoly—keeping them safe from those interest and excise penaltites. Compensation is presumed reasonable when:

1. the compensation arrangements are approved, in advance, by an authorized body of the exempt organization (for example, a national consulting firm) composed of independent individuals,

2. the board or committee obtained and relied upon appropriate data when making its decisions, and

3. the board or committee documented its decision-making process.

Intermediate Sanctions acts as an alternative to revoking the exempt status of an organization when disqualified persons receive an excess benefit. As an executive compensation consultant, I repeatedly conducted Intermediate Sanctions reviews for not-for-profit organizations. In addition to determining the competitiveness of compensation and benefits offered, we assessed the *reasonableness* of the compensation and benefits provided to disqualified persons to ensure compliance. Competitiveness and reasonableness are not one and the same.

For example, an Executive Director of a not-for-profit might receive compensation that trails the 50th percentile (or more closely mirrors the 25th percentile) and lacks competitiveness. However, according to Intermediate Sanctions regulations, the pay is deemed reasonable. Alternatively, the compensation offered might closely mirror the 75th percentile, well above the 50th percentile targets. The pay, internally, may exceed the organization's philosophy in terms of competitiveness, but remains reasonable under Intermediate Sanctions regulations.

> *Because of my company's reputation for integrity, we were hired to realign the programs of an organization that failed an IRC Intermediate Sanctions review. Being audited and failing is rare, and having opinion letters prior to an audit ensures safe harbor. Although the organization failed, it was really ahead of its time—using pay for performance practices that weren't common for its industry or its size relative to other employers. That is why it failed. If it had been compared to the for-profit sector, the practices would have been considered minimal at best (below market). Therefore, ensuring programs are competitive and reasonable annually is also critical because "reasonable" practices are constantly changing.*

Conclusion

Consultants educate, provide research and detailed analyses, and develop informed conclusions and recommendations regarding a company's compensation programs. Human Resources, senior leadership, the CEO, and Board members use the information to determine the pay programs and pay levels necessary to attract, reward, and motivate the talent needed to achieve the company's business strategies. The process is annual, iterative, and ongoing due to the constantly changing marketplace and business environment.

CHAPTER 3

Identify All the Players

In an interview with Denver Broncos quarterback Peyton Manning (previously of the Indianapolis Colts), he described how he prepares for games each week: He studies videos meticulously, and tries to understand each play and each team. As a result, he identifies their strengths and weaknesses. He prepares. Thoroughly.

"Game" implies players and a lack of consequences. "Game" implies fun and excitement. "Game" implies a beginning and an end.

"Game" *should* imply winners and losers. "Game" should imply opposing sides. "Game" should imply strategy, execution, alliances, and partnerships. "Game" should imply lack of emotions. "Game" should imply theory, practicality, and reality. "Game" should imply risk and rewards. "Game" should imply not only the opportunity to win but also the opportunity to win by a lot.

Executive compensation is a game. Not a fun game. Not a game for sport. Not a game with a beginning and an end, but a game that constantly repeats. A game that requires research, attention, maneuvers, and outcomes. Similar to football, executive compensation requires strategy, time, patience, and motivation. Unlike football, the same game constantly repeats unless you change employers or unless key players or business circumstances change.

The game includes many players, such as executives, Board members, institutional investors, key stakeholders, and public optics.

From 1995 to 2003, Richard Grasso led The New York Stock Exchange (NYSE) and is credited with transforming the NYSE into the preeminent trading institution and efficiently restarting operations after the 2011 terrorist attacks. Yet Grasso, the Board, and the NYSE experienced unexpected public humiliation when it was disclosed in August 2003 that Grasso's deferred compensation package totaled $140 million— a number that shocked the public. Following a blistering media storm and extensive public criticism, Grasso was asked to step down. A highly respectable career was quickly tarnished. There were lawsuits demanding repayment, and countersuits demanding contractual fulfillment. Grasso was eventually ordered to repay a large portion of his package because at the time of *the deferred compensation award, the NYSE was a nonprofit institution and this constituted excessive compensation. The public optics was worse than the actual accusations and penalties because Grasso was deemed a scoundrel, found guilty in a media trial before the actual trial occurred.*

The stakes are high in many organizations. Wealth accumulation or loss occurs easily. Significant wealth accumulation results from more than just base salary. Many additional rewards are calculated as a percentage of base salary—such as annual incentives, the value of long-term incentives (equity grants), benefits, and retirement income. A few percentage points equates to thousands or millions of dollars gained or lost.

Executive compensation is far more than a process. Compensation involves many people and players, including the community. For example, the CEO of a nonprofit once shared with me how her compensation package received first-page billing in the local paper before she started. The organization's key stakeholders comprised healthcare providers, employees, patients, and the community. Optics was critical to success because there were so many players in the game and each had different points of view and perspectives regarding her compensation. Additionally, she faced an uphill battle because the initial optics suggested she received too much money.

Every player is involved to varying degrees; each player does not retain equal power. In some organizations, the Board wields significant power; in others, shareholders rule; in still others, it's management. They key lies in identifying the players and understanding their influence. **By understanding your company's players and their degree of influence, you can develop a targeted strategy for your compensation package, regarding what to negotiate and whom to ask.**

You must understand every group that has a stake in the game, because executive compensation is a high-stakes game. Athletes have a coach; you have me.

The Players

Player Number 1: The Board of Directors

A Board of Directors consists of individuals who oversee a company's business activities. Overall, its responsibilities are typically detailed in the organization's bylaws, which also define the number of board members, how they are elected, when they meet, and so on. Board members oversee the company's strategic plan, monitor the CEO's (and other senior executives) performance, ensure financial prudence, approve budgets, report to stakeholders, and determine/approve the CEO's compensation (as well as that of his or her direct reports).

To establish the executive compensation program the Board of Directors' Compensation Committee approves the company's compensation philosophy, peer group, and CEO compensation. The CEO presents his/her recommendations for compensation regarding his/her direct reports, for the Committee's approval. The Committee presents the final plan and recommendations to the full Board. While the Board of Directors can consist of both outside directors (non-employees) and management, committee members are generally outside directors (this is mandatory for publicly traded companies). Most importantly, pay discussions should occur without management present to ensure open, constructive discussions and debate.

The important point to realize is that some Boards are more active than others. And some Boards create committees with the right expertise and knowledge, whereas other committees are young in their experience and require more ongoing education. Boards, admittedly, do not always execute the right decisions and therefore need to act expediently to remedy difficult situations. For example, J.C. Penney hired CEO Ron Johnson in 2012 to revamp the company. After one year of dismal performance results, the Board reduced his pay by 96 percent and then terminated his contract. Presumably this measure achieved two results: (1) It signaled the Board's control of the situation, and (2) it protected the Board from intense shareholder criticism and actions. The lesson the public learned: this Board exercises significant control over the company, its direction, and its compensation.

Board members are under close scrutiny from shareholders and government regulations that ensure the Board effectively and efficiently upholds their fiduciary responsibilities—especially those related to executive compensation. Although the "corporate shield" protects Board members from personal liability, major shareholders can demand their dismissal or shame them into resigning. For example, Yahoo! repeatedly hired short-term CEOs from 2009 to 2013, and by the time Marissa Mayer was hired, major shareholders demanded some Board members resign. During the financial crisis when Lehman collapsed, Boards were under intense public scrutiny for purportedly approving flawed compensation programs. J.P. Morgan Chase received a flurry of media attention regarding

its combined CEO/COB role—which shareholders had approved—and the perceived lack of independence that created.

> ○ *The Board of a major public firm wanted
> highly leveraged packages for the execu-
> tives. The Board members received the
> same highly leveraged package. Wall Street
> loved the leverage and when the company
> performed, the stock price soared.*

> ○ *Another public company Board wanted
> reasonable, competitive pay, but nothing
> that would land them on the front page
> of the WSJ. Their stock price stayed the
> same. The stock market doesn't necessar-
> ily reward conservative, but on the upside it
> didn't go down from aggressive compensa-
> tion decisions.*

> ○ *A not-for-profit Board was reluctant to ap-
> prove pay above the 25th percentile be-
> cause they wanted to manage optics and
> act conservatively. The downside here is
> that the nonprofit could potentially lose
> talented people because it wasn't willing
> to pay more. This conservative approach
> could cause more harm than good.*

> ○ *A pre-IPO Board (composed mostly of
> passive investors) remained inactive in the
> compensation process, allowing the CEO
> to exert full control over compensation
> decisions. This is not what highly effective
> Boards or management teams desire. It*

does not lead to productive, robust discussions or decisions.

In each organization, understanding the Board's role—especially at the executive level—proves critical when developing compensation strategies. Whether or not the Board's interests need to be recognized and considered will vary from firm to firm.

Player Number 2: Major Shareholders

Major shareholders are individuals or firms with majority, or at least significant voting power. These shareholders can act like a silent owner or an extremely active participant in the company's operations. Carl Icahn is one of the more well-known major shareholders/activists/investors in multiple corporations. When warranted, Icahn wields his axe to either demand change or buy more shares and assume full control to execute change. Icahn has assumed substantial or controlling positions in various corporations, including RJR Nabisco, TWA, Texaco, Phillips Petroleum, Western Union, Viacom, Uniroyal, Marshall Field's, Marvel Comics, Revlon, Federal-Mogul, Fairmont Hotels, Blockbuster, Time Warner, and Motorola. Icahn repeatedly pursues corporate change:

- In 2004, Icahn purchased a large block of stock of Mylan Laboratories and, after Mylan had announced a deal to acquire King Pharmaceuticals, Icahn threatened a proxy fight over the acquisition because he felt the deal required Mylan to overpay.
- Icahn owned about 3.3 percent of Time Warner, worth billions. Icahn demanded additional action

to increase shareholder value. On February 7, 2006, Icahn and a group of other investors called for the breakup of Time Warner into four companies and the creation of stock buybacks totaling approximately $20 billion. Ten days later, Icahn's group agreed not to contest the reelection of the board members if Time Warner would buy back up to $20 billion of stock, nominate more independent Board members, and significantly cut costs.

◑ In 2008, Icahn pressed Yahoo! to oust Jerry Yang as CEO.

Major shareholders such as Icahn can demand their interests be upheld at any time, especially regarding pay and Board member selection. Because of their ownership, they can wield significant power and influence.

> *During the late 1990s/early 2000s I consulted with a company in which Icahn was a major investor. While we were designing and implementing a bankruptcy and emergence compensation plan, Icahn was attempting a corporate takeover. The compensation programs could not be assessed or redesigned until the financial structure of the organization was settled.*

Understanding the potential influence of major shareholders unearths insights into which business strategies—and therefore what underlying compensation goals—are important. A corporate takeover during a bankruptcy radically alters the compensation strategy and approach. Therefore it would alter a powerhouse's approach. **By understanding the business**

strategy, powerhouses can better align their performance to the financial goals of the organization.

Player Number 3: Executives

As discussed in Chapter 1, executives establish the company's short- and long-term business plan, oversee its implementation, and are typically responsible for the company's P&L (profit and loss) or its major functions, such as Human Resources. These are generally single-incumbent roles with extensive strategy-setting and decision-making autonomy.

The level of influence executed by executives depends on three key factors:

1. The specific role and the strategic importance of this role to the organization at any moment in time

2. Performance

3. Individual factors (a.k.a. perception)

For example, a Head of HR may wield the same level of influence as the head of a major P&L depending on the individuals. Conversely, a CFO may be viewed as a critical business partner or as the "accountant on board."

Executives may also be privy to—or influence—the actual compensation design or award payouts. Aligning oneself with the right executives will always help influence a person's financial payouts. For example, if an annual incentive plan includes the achievement of predetermined performance objectives as well as the achievement of subjective measures (such as management by objectives), discussions with executives can positively (or negatively) influence the payouts of the subjective measures. Let's assume you are a senior-level manager within a firm that pays bonuses based on the achievement of financial and subjective performance measures. Your boss, an executive, meets with his/her direct reports to discuss year-end performance annually. How your boss perceives that performance will influence the payout of your annual incentive payout (bonus).

Alternatively, consider when executives present the overall achievement of performance measures to the Board—seeking approval of the bonus plan payout. These executives exercise significant influence over the total plan funding and its subsequent payouts.

During times of financial crisis, industry changes, or business threats, executives can exercise significant compensation demands in order to be enticed to save the sinking ship. For example, in the early 2000s, the telecom industry underwent major consolidation and many companies went bankrupt. Working in Washington, D.C. at the time, where there was a plethora of telecom companies, provided me with ample clients who needed help engaging and retaining employees. Retention programs became the norm for key employees. Payments could be structured in numerous ways: paid based on time (50 percent in two months and 50 percent upon the business closing) or performance (50 percent upfront and 50 percent upon a successful bankruptcy emergence). Employees able to stomach the risk could receive substantial payouts if successful.

Player Number 4: The Federal Government

The federal government plays an active role *re*acting to public outcry. Historically, regulators pass laws intended to curb executive compensation and quiet public discord. Here are some examples of when government regulators reacted to public outcry (or financial insolvency) with the intent to curb executive compensation:

○ *Example 1*: In 1984, Congress taxed golden parachutes (compensation provided to executives due to a change in control and, potentially, termination) if the resulting windfall exceed three times base salary. Prior to 1984, parachute payments were rare. However, after 1984, these payment provisions became more common, with the norm then set at three times salary.

○ *Example 2:* In 1992, the SEC required companies to increase disclosure. As a result, salaries increased because companies knew what their peers paid and what they would need to pay to be competitive.

○ *Example 3:* In 1993 Congress capped the deduction for cash salary at $1 million while exempting "performance-based" stock options. The result? CEO salaries approached $1 million in cash. Today, base salaries above $1 million are common and companies no longer consider the deduction.

○ *Example 4:* In 2003, the Financial Accounting Standards Board (FASB) finally required the expensing of stock options. Therefore, there was a significant increase in restricted stock grants. Restricted stock grants provide significant compensation and leverage but require less equity from the company (and have a lower dilutive effect). Conversely, overall eligibility decreased to manage grant levels. Companies had to employ other rewards (or just explain the lower overall compensation levels) to replace the perceived value lost from potential grants.

Compensation consultants and companies pay close attention to current trends and regulations. Programs are designed, evaluated, and redesigned to comply with current regulation. Optics can be a powerful motivator for many organizations to ensure a positive reaction from employees, shareholders, and the public. In terms of being an active player, the federal government's regulations may impact program design but generally not compensation decisions or award determinations.

For nonprofits, however, the federal government is more of an active player because the IRS can legally review a 501(c)(3)'s or (c)(4)'s compensation provided to a disqualified person to determine whether the pay is reasonable. If the pay is deemed unreasonable and excessive, an intermediate sanction is imposed, such as an excise tax. Therefore many nonprofits engage outside consultants to conduct Intermediate Sanctions reviews to confirm the pay is reasonable.

Player Number 5: Stockholders

A stockholder or shareholder is an individual or institution (including a corporation) that legally owns a share of company stock. Publicly traded stock usually confers the right to buy or sell shares, vote on the directors, and propose shareholder resolutions. Stockholders may propose proxy rules asking for shareholders to vote against the company's compensation programs.

However, recent regulations require public companies to seek shareholder approval rather than just address disapproval.

"Say on Pay" refers to the governance procedure allowing shareholders to vote their approval on the remuneration (compensation and benefits) provided to a company's executives. Part of the Dodd-Frank Act, the law supposedly provides investors and shareholders with more accountability and transparency. Acting as a check and balance system, "Say on Pay" refers to the purview shareholders have when it comes to reviewing executive compensation. Although Board members have a fiduciary responsibility to the company to ensure competitive—yet fair—compensation practices, "Say on Pay" allows shareholders to vote as well.

All public companies in the United States are required to periodically submit their compensation plans to a "Say on Pay" vote by shareholders, at least once every three years. Most corporations pass. According to a study conducted by Semler Brossy Consulting Group in 2012, 91 percent had a vote pass with at least 70 percent shareholder approval. Of the 2,215 companies in the Russell 3000 index that were surveyed, only 2.6 percent (57 companies) failed. Of the 57 companies that failed to pass, two of the CEOs were female at the time the compensation was disapproved—Heather Bresch of Mylan Inc., and Patti Heart of International Game Technology Company.[1] Interestingly, although there isn't a correlation between "yes" votes and market value, there are trends by industry. Telecom received the most shareholder support (100 percent) while healthcare received the least (93 percent).

In some of the most recent losses, Citigroup shareholders negated CEO Vikram Pandit's $14.8 million package after a 44.3 percent stock decline 2011. Shareholders also voted overwhelmingly against (4:1) the $5.8 million pay package

Chiquita Brands awarded CEO Fernando Aguirre following a 41 percent decline in its stock price. Typically, shareholders contest executive compensation when the stock price lags significantly and when their expectations are mismanaged. A rejected say-on-pay vote requires the company to revise its compensation programs. If programs are not realigned, shareholder activists oversee campaigns to unseat or discredit compensation committee members who don't respond to the shareholder disapproval.

Boards and management both now hire executive compensation consultants to review, analyze, and approve plans. Proxy advisors such as the Institution of Shareholder Services (ISS) also advise companies regarding shareholder practices and how to secure "yes" votes. Transparency and accountability is paramount. Therefore, if you work for a public company, your firm may employ not one but two outside firms to review and analyze the executive compensation programs offered.

Player Number 6: The Judicial System

The judicial system, generally of the state where the company is incorporated, is actively involved in compensation systems only during bankruptcy filings and bankruptcy emergence. The judicial system approves or denies a proposed compensation program for companies that file bankruptcy. Companies that file Chapter 11 under the Internal Revenue Code must seek approval for all special compensation programs during the bankruptcy period, including retention grants and severance payments. The bankruptcy court can approve, ask for additional information, request revisions, or deny proposed programs. Consultants work with the bankruptcy courts to develop programs that meet the needs of all interested parties, including debtors.

Player Number 7: Employees

Different employee cultures necessitate different pay programs to attract, retain, and motivate a workforce that achieves the company's short- and long-term business objectives. Here are some examples of this:

- A high-growth culture with a younger workforce might require more competitive pay packages (and limited benefits).

- A mature company culture consisting of an older workforce would require more robust benefits and, potentially, a retirement plan.

- A culture of high turnover (such as retail) requires market pay, significant people management, and benefits that may not start until after 60 days on the job, to avoid enrollment costs for individuals who don't stay too long.

- Not-for-profit employees generally focus on the mission. They should receive average pay and fairly good benefits but no long-term incentives; they manage to a budget rather than to profits or operating performance, so long-term incentives are uncommon. Therefore, the executives don't typically receive above-average pay, excessive perks, or long-term incentives either.

- During a restructuring, employees have leverage—they are needed to ensure a smooth transition.

Retention programs become imperative for key employees needed to manage the firm through the restructuring process. To safeguard against losing employees who want to find safe employment elsewhere before the doors officially close, companies design and grant retention programs.

Employees matter. Consider the hypothetical XYZ Company. Let's say that, historically, XYZ's employees have exhibited long tenure and loyalty. The prestige of working for XYZ (and receiving XYZ stock) trumped most other forms of compensation, both tangible and intangible. But recently, with new leadership, XYZ's product launches have faltered, its prestige weakened. Now, XYZ employees have started submitting resumes in historic numbers and exploring options elsewhere. Therefore, retention programs might become a more important part of the compensation program for XYZ employees and its executives.

In some companies, employees exercise leverage as a group. These employees vote on many of the programs offered throughout the company. But in most companies the leverage is exercised at the individual level, based on the individual's ability to perform above expectations, generate significant profits, or excel at a role that is strategically important. At XYZ, high-performing employees—critical to the future success of this hypothetical organization—exercise significant leverage.

Also, employees able to design the next great thing, market the next great thing, or deliver the next great thing also wield leverage. That is why perception is critical.

You Need To Know Which Players Have Power

After identifying the players, it is important to identify and acknowledge their degree of influence with a company. Not all players are present at every compensation "game" within every company or industry, and not all players exhibit the same degree of influence at any point in time.

To determine where the influence lies, assess your own company. When analyzing your own organization, list the following key pieces of information:

1. **Industry**
   - For-profit or not-for-profit?
   - High-growth industry, mature industry, or declining industry?

2. **Stage of growth**
   - Pre-IPO/start-up?
   - Early stage, mature, or declining?
   - Ripe for merger or acquisition?

3. **Size**
   - Number of employees

4. **Board member composition**
   - Are there any venture capitalists or significant majority shareholders?
   - How many are outside directors (non-employee directors)?

5. **Number of senior (truly the top) executives**
   - How many are female, and in what roles?

6. **Financial performance**
   - ◑ Understanding the company's financial situation sheds light on the degree of influence different plays wield.
   - ◑ In the past three years, how has revenue and stock grown?
   - ◑ What has been the EBITDA performance in the past three years?

Let's return to the XYZ example. Assume the answers are as follows:

Item	Description
Industry	Technology
Stage of growth	High growth but entering mature stage
Size	65,000 employees
Board member composition	7 inside and 1 outside; only 1 female
Number of senior executives	10 individuals, all white males

Item	Description
Financial performance	<ul><li>4-year revenue growth: 260%</li><li>4-year profit growth: 240%</li><li>4-year operating income growth: 450%</li><li>4-year EBIT: 420%</li><li>4-year stock price appreciation: 250%</li></ul>

Understanding financials and performance is paramount—or at least equally important as gauging influence. Being able to link your role's accomplishments to key performance measures signifies your understanding of the business. You will be deemed as "compatible" and as a leader because you understand the business.

Really understand the business.

And you know how to execute decisions that are in the company's best interest long-term.

In our XYZ example, the company has achieved significant financial performance in the past four years. And, even in a white-male dominated company, a woman with significant performance and the ability to appropriately discuss and tout her performance should achieve financial gains and exceptional wealth accumulation.

The level of influence could be determined as follows:

Player	Level of Influence (Low, Medium, or High)	Reasoning
Board of Directors	High	Leading company during time of transition and significant market competition.
Major Shareholders	Low	No shareholder has majority control.
Executives	High	Some individual executives are critical to company success in this time of significant market competition; they created the exceptional growth achieved.
Federal Government	Low	Government cannot influence or control pay at this company.
Stockholders	High	Stock price has never split. Executives want to align performance with total shareholder return. Need to deliver returns to stockholders.
Judicial System	Low	Company financially profitable. No current Mergers & Acquisitions prospects. No anti-trust issues.

Player	Level of Influence (Low, Medium, or High)	Reasoning
Employees	Medium	Depends on individual abilities and strategic importance to company, although, as a group, certain functions probably entertain a great deal of leverage depending on their role and impact on strategy execution.

XYZ Company may believe in providing all employees with stock options, but at the executive level, where diversity lapses, a woman at that table should be able to wield more power. This may seem counterintuitive, but, again, consider optics. You may know that XYZ wants female leadership to signal the importance of diversity, tenure, and work-life balance to its workforce. And, above all else, XYZ values ingenuity, creativity, and performance. A female leader who plays to the influencers, shows how her work increases shareholder value, aligns with key executives, *and* can articulate how she achieved those objectives increases her negotiating power at XYZ tenfold.

Conclusion

To adequately assess the "game" and how to play, understanding the players and their influence proves critical to success. You need this information to develop a targeted approach, and understand whom to ask, what to ask, when to ask, and how to ask for it. Now we will see how your powerhouse personality influences the outcomes, and how to use information—such as the information we developed for XYZ corporation—to your advantage.

CHAPTER 4

Female Powerhouses: The 4 Types

"Do not confuse my pleasant disposition with lack of resolve. If I have to have someone's head on a stick, I will."
—Female CEO of a health system

And by the end of the week, she did.

This CEO described her management philosophy (the
above quote) during our first meeting. I have never forgotten it.
She conveyed this philosophy during an off-site meeting shortly
after starting as CEO. She further explained her philosophy of
treating people with kindness and respect while expecting loyalty, commitment, and exceptional performance.

Read the quote again. Say it in a quiet voice, a loud voice,
an angry voice, and a disenchanted voice. Which voice makes

you feel respected? Humbled? Energized? Scared? When this executive made the statement, she used a quiet, polite, yet stern tone. She struck me as the type of person who never raised her voice, or got ruffled or flustered. She was confident and pleasant in her approach, yet firm.

Female executives such as this are powerhouses. They are paving the way for future women climbing the corporate ladder. Although we don't always subscribe to their approach or their performance, they fulfill a role future women may desire. And we can do nothing if we can't learn from our predecessors. Most of these women are succeeding. They achieve levels of success and career aspirations that were distant dreams decades ago. They garner compensation levels historically reserved only for men. And they lead—or intend to lead—major corporations that have significant economic impact on the global economy.

After advising hundreds of companies, I had the privilege of interacting with these female trailblazers. Though the ratio of female to male executives was low, it was inspiring to meet these women. I admired their perseverance, backgrounds, commitment, experiences, and insights. With each new client, I capitalized on the opportunity to absorb their lessons, pearls of wisdom, and leadership styles. Most importantly, I studied their professional personas.

Personally, female executives can be as different and unique as fingerprints. We all espouse characteristics that change with the ebb and flow of the tide. But when executives and aspiring leaders walk through their office doors, their professional personalities assume control. Like any superhero, female professionals have a secret identity. This secret identity is their personal/home identity. The professional identity is what colleagues see, feel, and hear, Monday to Friday.

One company knowingly delivered below market (50th percentile) pay to the majority of its executives. The CEO (a male) received compensation that was closer to market. The COO (a woman) was a high performer and strong leader with long tenure. She performed high-profile roles such as attending PR events and speaking at events on behalf of the organization. Her pay, however, was below market—below even a reasonable range. She asked for more but was presumed to be a low flight risk. Through time, she slowly received pay raises to bring her pay within a range of reasonableness, but it took time.

Putting aside individual personality differences, I observed four prevailing professional personalities, or leadership styles, that spanned each industry and company. The four prevailing personality styles are:

1. Assertive
2. Confident, yet humble
3. Politically savvy
4. Fiercely loyal

Whether consulting with Fortune 500 firms, IPOs, pre-IPOs, start-ups, not-for-profits, or private firms, the female executive personalities I met generally fell into one of the four categories. Some women personified all these characteristics throughout their careers, and others portrayed one personality in the beginning of their career and then evolved into others as their careers evolved.

It is management's *perception* of each personality that proved eye-opening.

As you now understand, my role as an executive compensation consultant included conducting analyses and providing the tools necessary for senior management and Board members to make educated compensation decisions. CEOs and Boards use these tools to discuss individual performance and determine compensation levels. What I discerned after almost 20 years of this is that how females are *perceived* impacts their compensation levels. In other words:

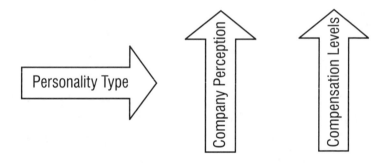

I am not suggesting that compensation is a popularity contest; being liked does not equal more money. But perception is 90 percent of reality, and determining compensation levels is not an exact science. There is a range of reasonableness associated with each award. Salary levels "target" the market, and individuals are paid within a range around these levels based on several factors. Compensation is based on individual factors such as experience, performance, and the impact of the role on the organization. How positively or negatively these factors are viewed can depend on the individual's personality and approach. In turn, these views impact the compensation levels offered and the awards earned.

Keep this important link in mind as you read the descriptions of each personality style in this chapter. As you review each personality and think about your own characteristics or characteristics of other female leaders, remember that women may exhibit aspects of each category, but that one category typically dominates. The next chapter (Chapter 5) further illuminates each personality as it relates specifically to compensation strategies—its advantages and disadvantages, and how to maximize the positives.

It is important to note that one personality is not better than another when it comes to maximizing compensation: Being confident yet humble does not trump an assertive personality, nor does a fiercely loyal powerhouse trump a politically savvy powerhouse. *All* of these personalities are powerhouses. Women should leverage their personalities appropriately to improve their pay levels, *not* try to be something they aren't.

The Assertive Powerhouse

Leaders need to be assertive when promoting new ideas, selling unpopular ideas, gaining buy-in, conveying decisions (popular or unpopular), and executing strategy. By definition, "speaking up" means being assertive. But in this circumstance, assertive powerhouses are assertive all the time, in every aspect of their professional roles. Some cultures require—even demand—assertiveness more than others.

At a high-growth, prestigious, Fortune 500 institution, I interviewed the Head of Operations—a woman. During our meeting, she was clear, concise, and definitive in her answers. She was not loud or overly conversational; she did not make small talk. She spoke intelligently and pointedly. She did not prepare prior to our meeting, but she didn't have to. She was clearly bright and could think on her feet. She was not condescending but conveyed an aura of confidence. Later, I learned about her group's stellar performance. Prior to meeting the other executives, I recognized she was highly regarded in this organization.

Within this company, her assertiveness was driven—and necessitated—by the culture. In another organization, one that emphasized soft skills, she might have appeared gruff, cold, or caustic. However, this company achieved Fortune 500 status and global brand recognition within a few short years. Their culture also incorporated accountability and teamwork. In hindsight, I now realize she recognized that teamwork was a secondary, or underlying corporate culture. She understood the need to promote herself and that it was an "up or out" culture—if she didn't perform, she would be fired.

Being "assertive" refers to how female executives present themselves, execute roles and responsibilities, and implement program changes. In other words, I do not mean "bitchy." Being assertive and being mean are not the same thing, and one does not imply the other. Simply put, assertive powerhouses do not fear sticky or sensitive situations or outcomes. These powerhouses forge forward—and some forge forward very pleasantly and kindly. When they proceed, however, their main objective is to get their point across.

I recently met an assertive powerhouse who was exceptionally kind and nice. She entered the room, immediately introduced herself to everyone, and joined the conversation without hesitation. She exhibited a pleasant, kind disposition. After someone gave a toast, she immediately stood up to give her own toast. She spoke her mind, yes, but in a kind yet firm manner. I liked her immensely.

Assertive powerhouses understand how to assume control, strongly responding to other assertive personalities without fear, and attacking complex or sensitive issues immediately while being straightforward in their approach.

Let me clarify with examples:

- A strong handshake versus a crippling handshake
- Providing commentary and opinions, even if not directly asked
- Assuming opinions will be accepted and followed
- Identifying issues and implementing changes
- Great problem solvers
- Addressing even sensitive issues head-on
- Expecting similar behavior from staff
- Interrupting colleagues to propel the conversation forward, to either offer examples of similar situations or to offer suggestions (assertive personalities can become frustrated with other people's inability to offer opinions, make decisions, or move forward)

◯ Confronting individuals without necessarily considering other options; the straightforward approach employed is generally the same approach
in all situations

◯ Very willing to talk it out—now

Some companies and industries mandate assertive personalities. For example, highly intense Wall Street firms that are
high-stakes and high-rewards promote assertive personalities.

> *We worked with one client to manage and im-
> plement a new base salary structure for 5,000
> employees. This firm espoused a high-pressure
> environment. The client, a female head of com-
> pensation, exuded the same characteristics.
> She addressed all issues head-on in order to
> effectively implement the change with minimal
> business disruption. Her boss, equally as asser-
> tive, constantly demanded updates. Errors were
> considered career-limiting at best. She man-
> aged her boss and the project within her culture
> by conducting meetings and conference calls
> daily, requesting updates, asking for opinions
> (when necessary), and making decisions by the
> end of each call.*

Assertive powerhouses promote their beliefs and defend
their opinions; however, they are willing to listen and learn
as well. Being assertive does not trump being self-aware. They
value other people's feelings and opinions, but believe strongly in
their own opinions. Their intent may not be malicious but they
can sometimes be perceived negatively if the other personalities

are less dominating. Assertive personalities can hug and talk it out, but prefer to follow a logical route and execute efficiently. Common traits of assertive personalities include: confidence, courageousness, decisiveness, endurance, initiative-taking, coolness, candidness, competence, commitment, and self-discipline.

Summary of the Assertive Powerhouse

Positive	Less Positive
▪ Not afraid of social interactions ▪ Able to tout their own performance ▪ Sell themselves well ▪ Willing to get the work done ▪ Very reliable	▪ May not always stop to listen ▪ Focus on outcomes and sometimes need to focus on process ▪ Can be impatient with obstacles that impede progress ▪ May not always want to consider other people's feelings

The Confident, Yet Humble Powerhouse

I coined the term *humble confidence* for an article published by MSN Careers that was cited multiple times in the Web sphere.[1] In it, I explained that humble confidence shines as knowledge, humility, skilled oral and written communication, friendliness, and appreciation. Female executives employ humble confidence to succeed in many organizational cultures. Humble confidence commands respect and appreciation for effective, efficient, consistent decision-making that is communicated in a respectful yet firm manner. Humble confidence opens the doors for feedback and new ideas. Humble confidence acknowledges various points of view, when appropriate. And humble confidence receives unsolicited accolades for stellar operational performance from peers and subordinates.

> *One female CEO I met led a healthcare organization. She was specifically hired to grow their marketplace and enhance their image and position in their surrounding communities. Considering that several large competitors were pounding on their door, this was a tall order. Her organization was navigating many diverse stakeholders, so change would be more challenging to execute. Her Board was focused on transparency and accountability, and comprised individuals hesitant to stretch their comfort zone with regard to strategy. This CEO established and executed a growth strategy while being mindful of the many stakeholders and the Board's needs. She worked within her parameters, not against them.*

Humble confidence is evidenced by:

⟍ Governing a meeting, its agendas, and its process in a kind manner, without losing control, creating isolation, or being overrun by strong personalities. These leaders solicit feedback and heed advice but make expedient and effective decisions that move the process—and company—forward. They communicate the reasons behind the decision to improve comfort levels and gain consensus.

⊙ An understanding of the company's culture. These leaders recognize what change to implement, how much, and when.

⊙ Commanding control of personal emotions. Female executives exhibiting humble confidence set aside personal feelings when making and communicating decisions. They also react appropriately to various situations, without overreacting. Their tone, demeanor, and word choice highlight their ability to handle stressful situations.

⊙ Considerate decision-making. These women understand when to gather input, how to use it, and how to effectively make decisions and follow through.

⊙ More deliberate approaches: options are considered and weighed before handling or addressing a situation. Other people's feelings are considered and highly valued.

⊙ An understanding that they can do the job—and do it well—but are not self-promoting.

This same CEO, when hired, was confronted with the challenge of needing to establish a productive working relationship with the COB. The COB had a considerable degree of influence that she needed to redirect. She worked with his personality and within the purview of her role to develop and execute the strategy and gradually shifted his frame of mind to becoming her most vocal advocate.

Humble confidence requires and desires emotional intelligence. These personalities employ techniques like emotional intelligence to govern their leadership. Female executives with high degrees of emotional intelligence understand and manage both their own emotions and the emotions around them. They know what they're feeling, what this means, and how their emotions can affect other people. Unlike an assertive personality, humble confidence accounts for others' feelings and perceptions more frequently. Common traits of Confident, yet Humble Powerhouses include: confidence, courage, integrity, decisiveness, initiative, maturity, candor, sense of humor, competence, commitment, creativity, self-discipline, and humility.

Summary of the Confident, yet Humble Powerhouse

Positive	Less Positive
▪ Understands own ability to perform and meet/exceed expectations ▪ Recognized by others as a role model and positive team member ▪ Willing to work with others in terms of their agenda/timeline	▪ Doesn't tout own successes often enough or at the right times ▪ Patient (sometimes too patient) with "the system" ▪ Willing to earn less to avoid rocking the boat

The Politically Savvy Powerhouse

Being politically savvy is a quality exhibited by many leaders. Engaging—and mastering—office social interactions require self-awareness, time, and energy. As an executive, office politics translates into power and influence. Politically savvy executives roam the field and walk the halls. They invest time interacting with peers as well as direct reports. They are visible. They play the game well—listening, developing friendships and advocates, creating cross-department alliances, and positioning their team and their work positively within the company. These executives use social interactions to create a shield against economic downturns and to reap rewards during periods of superior performance. Many aspiring leaders exhibit these same qualities.

Political savvy is evidenced by:

- Identifying both the internal and external politics that impact a company, and channeling the information to solve problems using both concrete and intangible data

- Approaching each situation with a clear perception of organizational and political reality that recognizes the impact of alternative courses of action (the difference between selling the *best* solution and the *right* solution that will be accepted by the majority)

- Soliciting opposing viewpoints by reading newspapers, books, and other publications with comprehensive analyses or exposing oneself to opposing viewpoints for the purpose of appearing open-minded

- Investing time to interact with peers in different departments and at different levels for the purpose of understanding the business better and forging allies

- Communicating decisions that either take different views into account or acknowledge the different viewpoints that might exist

- Reading people's nonverbal cues as well as verbal cues and adjusting her own behavior accordingly

During one industry client's Board meeting, there was a woman who led much of the discussion. She spoke intelligently, clearly, and succinctly. She did not overrun anyone, but she was clearly quite intelligent. She seemed to have a close rapport with most of the men. In fact, the men deferred to her. One thing I noticed was that she treated me with respect as well. Men, generally, treated me respectfully. Women, on the other hand, sometimes viewed me as young or as a threat. I often had to win the women over but much less so the men. This particular woman was confident. She prepared for each meeting thoroughly and came with thoughtful, educated questions and suggestions. She directed her questions right at me and asked for my opinion. Then she took my answers and made a decision, which she proposed to the Board. I think it was her internal confidence and respect for others that fueled her political savvy. This woman clearly wielded both power and influence. I recognized that she understood the importance of relationships and information and knew how to use both, because all of her proposals were accepted.

Playing the game is crucial to career success because manipulating social interactions is how power and influence are managed in any company. *Manipulating* social interactions sounds Machiavellian, but the outcome of effective social interactions is strong alliances and advocates within an organization. Social interactions act like an umbrella plan, offering coverage on rainy days, but do not guarantee advancement. If all else is equal, being politically savvy will propel an individual forward. However, if performance slides but the executive is politically savvy, then the individual is more likely to have job security. Political savvy alone does not guarantee success. Performance is still paramount.

Female executives who masterfully execute social interactions with other executives and wield significant power and influence within an organization are politically savvy.

I worked with a female executive who espoused political savvy. As a leader of a global consulting firm, she received rapid promotions and led major divisions and global practices within the firm. The firm experienced stages of both growth and decline, and during restructuring and downsizing she managed to land a more complex role. She had allies and advocates across the firm, in various divisions and practices. Even when the firm merged with another

company, she received a senior-level role lead-
ing a practice.

Sometimes female executives view political savvy as relationship-building or networking. However, this is only partly correct. Relationship-building or networking is not political savvy when it is underdeveloped or one-way.

Underdeveloped

I knew a senior female executive who vehemently pursued relationship-building as a means of bonding with clients/customers and expanding relationships, therefore generating business (revenue/sales). She asked personal questions and offered assistance with personal issues such as finding babysitters, doctors, and schools. Being a resource was her way of building relationships. The questions were a means to an end—fishing for issues she could solve easily. This can be effective, if used appropriately.

Sometimes her resources were not solicited. The question seemed to exist only because the female powerhouse asked—it wasn't freely offered. She sometimes offered solutions *un*solicited because she mistook politeness for acceptance. And the issues she solved were not critical—they helped personally but not professionally. Once she provided solutions that solved professional issues and helped clients solve their business issues, she cemented the relationship.

Relationships can be underdeveloped because they remain on a personal level. Relationship building—a business necessity—does not necessarily mean political savvy and business success. Relationship building does not mean roles will be protected during a downsizing or restructuring. Relationship-building needs to transcend the personal—to the professional—to be politically savvy.

Conversely, networking implies the development of professional relationships, in which individuals contact others for business reasons only, such as identifying career opportunities, discussing consulting offers, exploring new ventures, responding to job inquiries, requesting expertise, sourcing business deals, and so on. Whether online or in person, networking is a form of relationship-building. Using networking in a way that transcends the relationship beyond professional needs requires political savvy.

One-Way

Sometimes relationship-building can be one-way. Individuals help others (either personally or professionally) but receive nothing in return. The effort, in essence, is wasted. Being politically savvy means recognizing a value for your efforts—whether it is support, allies, friends, or business propositions. Female executives who continually write checks they can't cash engage in one-way relationship-building but are not politically savvy.

> *A few years ago I met a female executive at an academic institution. She told me that she loves "putting people together." This woman cited well-known alumni whom she connected with an investor. The result was a successful joint venture and company launch. She gained nothing from the connection personally*

or professionally (directly), but the institution received endowments. As a result, she gained advocates and allies throughout the institution.

Common traits of politically savvy leaders include: confidence, endurance, tact, coolness, maturity, assertiveness, sense of humor, creativity, flexibility, and empathy/compassion.

Summary of the Politically Savvy Powerhouse

Positive	Less Positive
• Great at networking and building relationships • Able to build networks outside of own business; in other divisions • Studies the culture and recognizes what can and cannot be done (and when) within the organization's limits	• Does not always network with the right people at the right times • Assumes other people will act appropriately as her spokesperson • Doesn't necessarily ask for more or insert herself in the compensation process; assumes others are taking care of her

The Fiercely Loyal Powerhouse

Loyal might seem counter to the term *powerhouse*. It isn't. In fact, the term describes incredibly powerful women who scale corporate ladders and assume complex roles, similar to their peers. However, these females climb the ladder at a normal rather than accelerated rate, and rarely question compensation. This powerhouse's attributes include understanding and patience, which leads to the ability to trust in other people and companies. For these "believing" powerhouses the trust is given first and freely, not necessarily earned. They are true believers—they believe in other people and their ability to meet expectations, fulfill roles and responsibilities, and deliver on their commitments. These powerhouses inherently believe the organization will "do the right thing."

They are devoted, working almost 24/7. Their sense of trust—and deep need to trust—overrules their belief in self-promotion. They refrain from self-promotion, to the point that they act embarrassed when others tout their performance. These powerhouses reason that the company is (or should be) aware of their dedication, performance, and leadership. They trust the company to act appropriately based on these facts. Extremely engaged, these powerhouses act as role models for other women. They are approachable, friendly, and almost maternal at work.

> *I worked with a female executive at a Fortune 500 firm with multiple divisions. She was extremely pleasant and friendly. Yet she wasn't overly assertive, confident, or politically savvy. She performed her job well and willingly assumed multiple projects or tasks beyond her normal job duties. She was a solid performer and very loyal—with long tenure.*

Fiercely loyal powerhouses are:

- Diligent—arrive early and stay late consistently
- Extremely loyal—usually have long tenure with one firm
- Active participants in meetings while not talking "over" people
- Humble—do not engage in active self-promotion
- Typically the go-to person for special projects because they get the job done
- Like a teapot—sometimes their top blows because they generally do not react (or overreact) to things
- Promoted in due course (not at an accelerated rate) and perform well at their roles
- Mentors—willing to train and develop other people and provide guidance

One female powerhouse espoused loyalty and engagement. Her fan club included the CEO, operational and functional executives, and direct reports. This particular female powerhouse knew everyone; she was personable and friendly and knew people's names. She was present. Visible. When a catastrophic weather-related event occurred, she was on the front lines, helping with recovery. She breathed the culture of the organization—she was the organization. As a result, when she talked, people listened. It is important to note, she did not always share her opinions. She weighed her options mentally and determined when to voice an opinion and when to defer. In fact, even when her opinions were specifically sought, she sometimes refrained from sharing if she deemed the situation too high-risk.

Because of their maternal attitude, fiercely loyal power-houses amass loyal supporters among direct reports and lower-level employees. Their leadership style accounts for other people's views, but these powerhouses ultimately forge decisions based on customer or company needs. Fiercely loyal power-houses seem like an "old dog" at first—afraid to learn new tricks. However, they are willing to learn and adapt. Common traits of fiercely loyal powerhouses include being honest and dependable, showing initiative, using tact, possessing integrity, acting unselfishly, and being competent and committed.

Summary of the Fiercely Loyal Powerhouse

Positive	Less Positive
• Other women look up to these powerhouses as role models • Loyal; have long tenure with companies • Develop robust, trust-based relationships with colleagues	• Would rather the company did the right thing instead of asking or rocking the boat • Very hesitant to leave an organization • Values other intrinsic rewards more than compensation (such as workplace flexibility), which the company can take advantage of

Comparison of the Personality Powerhouses

I'm sure you have noticed the overlap among the power-house personality types. At some point in time, each powerhouse personality may exhibit several of these traits, but one generally dominates. Using common leadership traits, the following table compares each personality.

Trait	Personality Powerhouse			
	Assertive	Confident, yet Humble	Politically Savvy	Fiercely Loyal
Confidence	X	X	X	
Courage	X	X	X	X
Decisiveness	X	X		
Sense of Justice				X
Endurance	X	X	X	X
Tact		X	X	X
Initiative	X	X	X	X
Coolness	X		X	
Maturity	X	X	X	X

Trait	Personality Powerhouse			
	Assertive	Confident, yet Humble	Politically Savvy	Fiercely Loyal
Assertiveness	X	X		
Candor	X			
Sense of humor			X	X
Competence	X	X	X	X
Commitment	X	X	X	X
Creativity		X	X	X
Self-discipline	X	X		X
Humility		X		X
Flexibility			X	X
Empathy/ Compassion		X		X

The Powerhouse Personalities and Organizational Culture

The most successful female executives I have encountered mirrored their professional identity to their company's identity. In other words, they were a good cultural fit for their companies. When both personality and leadership culture match, success and money follow more easily. If leadership espouses the same characteristics as a particular powerhouse, their perception improves. Naturally, we are all drawn to people who are *like* us.

Organizational psychologists define cultures using many terms, although there are four commonly accepted groupings: formal (or control), clan (or collaborative), creative, and competitive. The following table provides definitions for each major category.

Organizational Culture	Definitions
Formal	Hierarchical. Follow chain of command. Rules and procedures govern behavior.
Clan	Friendly place to work. People share a lot of themselves. Like a family. Leaders are considered parental figures. Group loyalty and sense of tradition are strong. Great importance is given to group cohesion.

Organizational Culture	Definitions
Creative	Entrepreneurial. Focus on innovation. Individual initiative and freedom encouraged. Few rules.
Competitive	Results-driven. People are goal-oriented. Emphasis on reputation, winning, and success.

Many different industries lend themselves to these four types of organizational cultures. They broadcast these characteristics regardless of factors such as growth stage, leadership, maturity, access to capital, or competition. For example, investment banking and consulting firms, regardless of the number of employees or their growth stage, have competitive organizational cultures. On the other hand, banks typically espouse formal cultures—they are process-oriented, hierarchical, and focus on rules and procedures. Within these industries, some companies may buck the trend because they are the industry leader, the risk-taker, or at a different stage of company maturity, or they have more or less access to capital.

Of course, organizational culture is more varied than only four types. Other characteristics define cultures as well:

- Innovative
- Stable
- People-oriented
- Outcome-focused
- Detailed

- Team-oriented
- Flexible
- Opportunistic
- Growth-oriented
- Risk-taking
- Careful
- Decisive
- Stable
- Predictable
- Fair
- Respectful
- Supportive
- Demanding
- Achievement-oriented
- Tolerant
- Calm
- Reflective
- Collaborative

An organization's culture may not remain constant. The culture may evolve with financial performance. In other words, when the money flows, people are happy. When it ebbs, people are stressed. But true cultural characteristics emerge—and are sustained—whether the company performs well or is flailing.

One client, a Fortune 500 firm, experienced tremendous growth, profitability, and financial success within an extremely short period of time. The founders grew the company, went public, and were a major industry contender within a few short years. Ostensibly, the culture was performance-driven. The firm's culture espoused innovation, outcomes, risk-taking, and entrepreneurial behavior. They promoted team work and collaboration. However, once the financial performance began to slide, the true culture emerged—one that was individualistic and extremely competitive. Although teamwork was still important, it was less important when times were tough.

Significant advantages and disadvantages are associated with each personality powerhouse regarding compensation. The advantages assume the organizational culture promotes that personality. With any of the powerhouse personalities I described, if the personality runs counter to the organization's culture, success will be limited or delayed if the powerhouse is unable to exploit the right facets of her personality. **Understanding how to maximize compensation means understanding this link.**

An obvious question at this point is, *Can these female powerhouses exist in company cultures that run 180 degrees counter to their personalities?* In other words, can they swim upstream and still be successful? Many companies can—and do—sustain all of these personalities. Company cultures are not defined the same way as the powerhouse personalities; there is a lot of overlap. Only companies with extremely strong, pervasive cultures that are driven top-down will be toxic to individuals with different viewpoints. So the short answer is yes, these powerhouses can exist in all organizational cultures. However, the degree of success will be based on the powerhouse's ability to *maximize the right aspects of her personality.* A more paternalistic culture might hire an assertive personality because change and growth are desperately needed—people need to get on board or leave. Some companies hire a specific type of person because it is what they think they need. However, if that person doesn't execute (achieve the desired performance), he or she will be terminated because the personality differences aren't worth the disruption to decision-making, leadership, and morale. What I am suggesting is that you need to leverage the aspects of your personality (the pros) to help you succeed and downplay the sides that might be limiting your successes. If a female power-house can do that, she can succeed.

Otherwise, if any powerhouse truly operates countercul-ture, one of two things can happen:

1. It isn't a good fit and therefore not a long-term situation.

2. The powerhouse doesn't progress upward in the firm.

Truly, the female powerhouse isn't happy in a culture that isn't a good fit. No one is. This conundrum applies to all peo-ple, male or female, executive or employee. If it isn't a good cultural fit, success will be limited. You may not get developed and/or you may find success difficult to achieve, and career happiness becomes elusive.

Here are some examples of the four powerhouses I've en-countered who operated counter-culture.

◑ **Assertive:** One client had a relaxed, team-oriented, innovative, casual, outcome-focused culture, where I interacted with an assertive woman. Brought in for her expertise, she identified the missing or incorrect processes and proceeded to implement unilateral change. This woman—extremely smart, polite, and intelligent—heeded her job but did not heed her organization's culture. Her fast and furious changes could not be absorbed that quickly. The CEO and COO had difficulty supporting her in light of the emotional chaos she was causing.

◯ **Confident, but Humble:** A financial services client had an extremely intelligent, educated, and confident female head of human resources. When I met her, I thought she was polite, friendly, knowledgeable, and well-liked. As mentioned previously, financial services firms espouse more assertive cultures. She expended considerable energy touting the performance of her group and her people, but, in my opinion, not enough time touting her own performance. This misstep caused her to limit the number of advocates and allies she garnered among her peers and superiors. While she exhibited a confident but humble personality, at the executive level, because she could not improve her perception about her ability to execute and effect change, she and the company separated ways.

◯ **Politically Savvy:** We advised a national, well-known not-for-profit where a new female CEO was hired to set a new course for the organization. The CEO established a strategic direction which was approved by the Board, but she failed to solidify relationships with some Board members. In essence, they approved the strategy but not her. Her heart was in the organization—she breathed the mission. She thought she had their support, but their relationship was really one-way rather than mutual.

She was politically savvy, but not necessarily with all the right people at the right time. Once there was a bump in the road, or the changes were slow to evolve, she became a scapegoat—sacrificed by the Board for the sake of public optics and appearances, regardless of her performance.

◑ **Fiercely Loyal:** We periodically worked with a company whose HR department remained relatively constant. In fact, throughout the course of our relationship, the same people held the same roles. At first I thought this signified loyalty and commitment in exchange for financial rewards. But upon closer inspection, I saw that the head of HR (male) was replaced with another male head of HR in that timeframe. The women who reported to that role were not promoted. Now I knew that other women in that organization were recognized and were receiving rapid promotions. Therefore the more I understood the women in this department, the more I realized they were running counterculture—not touting their performance enough to be progressed at a faster rate. They were loyal and high performers, but not able to break the leadership ranks because their personalities did not allow it.

Conclusion

The four female executive powerhouses (assertive, confident, politically savvy, and fiercely loyal) can exist in many organizational climates. Select companies may require more assertive personalities whereas others require more politically savvy personalities, but most companies can incorporate all of these powerhouses. Understanding your personality type—and how to leverage your personality within the company's culture—is critical to success, especially to maximize compensation.

That's the next step. You don't need to change your colors. You need to leverage the right aspects to succeed.

CHAPTER 5

Discover Your Powerhouse Personality

After reading about each powerhouse, you may have already identified your powerhouse personality. You may also be teetering between two powerhouses. A common reaction is, "It depends on the situation." Your powerhouse personality reflects the most common elements of a particular powerhouse most often and under most scenarios. It's important to realize this is not your "at home" identity. That is your secret identity. Your work personality is your powerhouse alter ego.

Your powerhouse personality may evolve and change as your career progresses. Sometimes our personality changes because we grow as individuals, due to intrinsic factors. Other times our powerhouse personality evolves because of external factors—experiences that happen to us during our professional careers. For example, a confident, but humble powerhouse might change if she is terminated due to a restructuring. She might become more politically savvy or assertive. A fiercely loyal powerhouse might become more assertive if her trust in her boss or employer is shattered. Perhaps she learned she was underpaid or not considered for a promotion. And a politically savvy powerhouse might become fiercely loyal if her relationships develop to the point that they are (a) long-term and (b) based on mutual trust.

This chapter briefly discusses five workplace scenarios and the most likely reactions from each powerhouse personality. The discussion should serve to further confirm which powerhouse personality best describes you—at least for now.

Scenario 1

You are in a sales role or have been asked to conduct cold-calls. You need to call potential customers and discuss a new product your company is offering. Your manager provides you with the names and contact information for 10 companies to contact by the end of today.

Assertive Powerhouse: Cold-calling is no sweat for this powerhouse personality. This powerhouse does not fear social interactions, so approaching unknown individuals to discuss a product or service does not ruffle her feathers. This personality would listen to the instructions, confirm the individuals to contact, and begin calling almost immediately.

Confident, but Humble Powerhouse: This powerhouse might pause at the thought of conducting cold calls. Approaching individuals without any prior relationship feels uncertain. To ensure success, this powerhouse might do research prior to making phone calls. The powerhouse might research the company and/or the individual and prepare for each phone call. The feedback received from one phone call would be used to strengthen the probability of success for subsequent calls.

Politically Savvy Powerhouse: Cold calling isn't nerve-wracking because politically savvy powerhouses enjoy building and leveraging relationships. This powerhouse might research the contacts to learn more about them in order to understand how to establish the connection, or to see if they know someone who can help make the introduction. Focusing on the relationship (rather than the product or service) is how this powerhouse approaches these situations.

Fiercely Loyal Powerhouse: Cold-calling does not excite a fiercely loyal powerhouse. In fact, cold-calling is the last thing she wants to do. In order to be successful, the fiercely loyal powerhouse might ask other powerhouses for tips and advice. This powerhouse thrives on developing genuine, long-term relationships based on trust. To build trust, this powerhouse does not want to appear "sales-y" or fake. Therefore, to be successful, this powerhouse will research and develop an approach that seems fair, reasonable, and genuine. The conversations might take longer (and this powerhouse might employ tactics enjoyed by Politically Savvy powerhouses for making connections) before the ultimate goal is achieved. However, process is just as important as outcome to this powerhouse.

Scenario 2

You are being interviewed for a new job. The job is a career switch and could be perceived as a bit of a stretch.

Assertive Powerhouse: The fact that the job is a career switch or a bit of a stretch does not phase this powerhouse. This powerhouse is prepared for potential questions and believes she has the skills to accomplish this role. She leverages past accomplishments to discuss how she would approach this job and be successful.

Confident but Humble Powerhouse: This powerhouse understands that the interviewer might have difficulty understanding why she would be a good fit. In fact, this powerhouse might even acknowledge that fear during the discussion. After acknowledging the fear, however, this powerhouse would explain why she is switching, how she has been successful in her previous career, and how she plans on being successful in the new job/role.

Politically Savvy Powerhouse: Before earning the interview, this powerhouse established connections at this firm. The interviewer most likely is already familiar with her and her accomplishments. Politically savvy powerhouses are chatty. As soon as she meets the interviewer, she is establishing a personal connection (perhaps through previous research or through conversation alone). When she's asked about her desire for a career switch or why the company should risk hiring her, she is prepared with answers. She may even suggest potential references for the interviewer to call to confirm her commitment and performance.

Fiercely Loyal Powerhouse: Switching careers is difficult for a fiercely loyal powerhouse. Just leaving the same company is challenging, let alone switching careers as well. This powerhouse thoroughly prepares for this interview, ready to answer questions regarding her career aspirations. She will reduce the perceived risk the potential employer would be taking by underscoring her commitment and desire to build long-term relationships. Through conversation and examples, this powerhouse establishes a mutual feeling of trust between her and the interviewer.

Scenario 3

The company is divesting the division in which you work. At a meeting with your manager, he discusses the divestiture, the process, and the fact that you will now be working for the new employer.

Assertive Powerhouse: Questions will flood an assertive powerhouse's brain. She may not be able to ask the questions—and wait for the answers—fast enough. The assertive powerhouse will want to understand all aspects of the transaction, the process, and her new role. She will ask about future job security. She will also ask about her compensation. No stone will be left unturned.

Confident but Humble Powerhouse: This news will derail a confident but humble powerhouse momentarily. Her confidence will be rattled because she wasn't asked whether she wanted to stay or go, or she wasn't valued enough (in her mind) to be retained. On the opposite end of the spectrum, she will feel reassured that she is being offered a job with the new company. She will process the news more slowly and ask pertinent questions. Upon more thought, she might return to the conversation with additional questions.

Politically Savvy Powerhouse: Presumably, this powerhouse is well-networked and the news did not come as a shock. Therefore she is prepared with thoughtful questions regarding the process and how she will be impacted. She will want to know with whom she can connect (as soon as possible) at the new firm.

Fiercely Loyal Powerhouse: This news derails a fiercely loyal powerhouse. She will be shocked because she did not make the decision to change—it was made for her. Whereas the fiercely loyal powerhouse will ask questions during the initial discussion, she will ask for time to digest the news and revisit the discussion. The fiercely loyal powerhouse may not automatically go with the new company. She may choose to ask for a severance package and look for a new role. Because her sense of trust in her current employer weakened, she is not willing to trust them with her future employment so easily.

Scenario 4

A new business meeting takes place between the powerhouse and several individuals from different companies. The individuals have been gathered to work together and address a challenging business situation.

Assertive Powerhouse: After the initial introduction, the assertive powerhouse approaches the different people in the room about what they do and what their experience is. She is interested in learning about them so she can understand their roles and how they relate to her role. If the company does not facilitate the discussion, the assertive powerhouse will assume this role in order to propel the conversation forward and make process decisions. Progress is important to this powerhouse.

Confident but Humble Powerhouse: This powerhouse will observe and learn the players. She will ask questions when appropriate but won't jump in as quickly as an assertive powerhouse. She recognizes her strengths and wants to understand other people's strengths and how everyone will work together. If the conversation lags, this powerhouse will facilitate and move the conversation along.

Politically Savvy Powerhouse: This situation does not intimidate a politically savvy powerhouse. She approaches this situation like all others—with the intent to learn individual motivations and develop mutually beneficial relationships. Based on her relationship with the company holding the meeting, she may already have background information and understand the players and their degree of influence. She is comfortable allowing others to run the meeting, displaying her confidence and expertise when appropriate. She secures lead roles that position herself more publicly with the company.

Fiercely Loyal Powerhouse: Establishing trust is critical for this powerhouse. She must believe the other parties will be trustworthy. Many of her initial questions will be about their experiences in similar situations. This powerhouse will facilitate the discussion but will only assume roles in which the chances of success are high. Put differently, she will minimize her risk of failure in this high-risk work situation. To ensure success of the entire project (in order to satisfy the client/

company), she may assume the role of task manager, ensuring all the parties are delivering as promised.

Scenario 5

It is time for your annual performance review. Your manager schedules a one-hour meeting to discuss your performance. You aren't sure how the conversation will go or how your performance will relate to your compensation.

Assertive Powerhouse: The assertive powerhouse will enter the meeting feeling friendly, calm, and ready to talk. Rather than wait for the manager to initiate the discussion, she will start with pleasantries and then begin to discuss performance. This powerhouse will help steer the discussion, focusing on what she perceives as her strengths and significant achievements. If areas for development are discussed, she will address those issues head-on, asking how she can improve, and when she can expect a raise (and how much) and promotion.

Confident but Humble Powerhouse: This powerhouse is fully aware of her performance and significant achievements for the past year. However, she isn't sure whether her manager is aware of each accomplishment. She will allow her manager to initiate the discussion but she may or may not discuss each accomplishment, allowing her manager to pick which ones to discuss. If areas for development are discussed, she will listen intently and quietly focus on how to improve.

Politically Savvy Powerhouse: Because these powerhouses typically have a good relationship with their managers, there are no surprises. If she feels her manager isn't aware of all of her accomplishments, this powerhouse might use this opportunity to raise awareness. The conversation will be pleasant and move along without awkward silences. Any potential areas for development will be discussed at a high level because the politically savvy powerhouse will know how to redirect the conversation. She will also empathize with her manager and her manager's work, digging for areas where she and her manager can work more closely together. This discussion is an opportunity for the politically savvy powerhouse to further her career. If no promotion is discussed, she will inquire about next steps and when she can expect a promotion.

Fiercely Loyal Powerhouse: This powerhouse expects to be rewarded for loyalty and performance. She will discuss the strengths mentioned by her manager but may not bring up additional accomplishments or strengths to discuss. She assumes the strengths that are discussed are the most important ones. She is willing to discuss areas for development and may or may not directly ask for promotions, more money, or career opportunities. If she believes she deserves a promotion or raise, she will ask. But she may not demand one.

Conclusion

These scenarios provide additional insights regarding each powerhouse's approach and thought process. Some powerhouses focus more on process (politically savvy and fiercely loyal) whereas others focus more on outcomes (assertive, and confident, but humble). Determining which powerhouse personality best describes you requires identifying which personality traits present themselves most often in most situations.

Most importantly, each powerhouse has strengths that, when leveraged appropriately, are formidable.

CHAPTER 6

Leverage Your Powerhouse Personality

Each female powerhouse personality shines in the workforce. However, sometimes the light shines so brightly that recipients, blinded, shield their eyes and look the other way. Other times the light doesn't shine brightly enough or in the right directions or at the right times. After 18 years in the executive compensation game, I have catalogued each personality's approach to compensation and chronicled successes and failures with each approach. The "failures" were not necessarily real failures, because these women were (and are) still respected and earned respectable levels of compensation. The "failures" just meant *limited successes* because these women could have earned more or been allocated additional responsibilities or accolades.

These limited successes can be broadened or converted into bigger successes. By marrying the *objective* (compensation philosophy, data gathering, structures and guidelines) with the *subjective* (impact of the individual on her compensation based on *perceived* experience, strategic impact, and/or performance), women can maximize their earnings. When I mention performance, I do not mean the quantifiable financial performance measures that must be achieved. Most plans have subjective measures as well—improving people-management skills, leveraging negotiating capabilities, partnering with colleagues in other lines of business to service clients, and so on. I am discussing the areas where the impact of someone's performance can seem bigger and greater based on how she is perceived.

You may be thinking that other people, both men and women, limit positive perception. You *may* believe that these people, men especially, minimize the impact of these contributions to lower pay levels. Not true. I will discuss this in greater detail in the next chapter, but for now here is the lesson: *most male colleagues are not consciously trying to limit the earnings capabilities of their female colleagues.* Men deliver or approve compensation they believe will be perceived as fair. They determine compensation awards based on company guidelines and what they believe would be considered appropriate.

The gap occurs in the definition of "fair." What is a fair increase (within the guidelines)? What is a fair equity grant (within the guidelines)? And even what constitutes fair severance (within the guidelines)? This is an importance difference between men and women: **what men believed they deserve and what women believe they deserved is hardly ever equal.** What women believe they deserve is usually *lower,* though it equals fair in their minds. Then others approve the award, believing they are delivering competitive pay levels and equitable pay. Women need to understand this discrepancy, exploit the right facets of their personality, and close the gap. If women believe they *should* earn more, they will be more likely to actually receive it.

Here are a few examples of the importance of perception:

> *The Head of Operations for the high-growth financial services firm with a pay-for-performance culture understood that performance was everything. Everything. She knew it was an "up or out" environment and that her tenure could be short if she didn't produce phenomenal results. Therefore when it came to pay, she came to the table prepared. She cited her performance, her impact on the bottom line, and the value she brought to the organization. In essence, without expressly saying it, she explained why she deserved above-market pay and additional equity. And she received it. She played her cards and she played to the company's strategic desires. The Board and management agreed because she delivered. She also inserted herself into the pay process rather than wait for the decision.*

Inserting oneself into the process is a first step. But it isn't enough. Being a passive player will not influence the outcomes. You need to be an active player.

> *The VP of Compensation and Benefits—an outstanding woman—was a fiercely loyal powerhouse. She was highly valued and an invaluable member of the leadership team, yet she wasn't receiving above-market pay until a new CEO decided she should be earning more. The previous*

CEO was not purposely trying to limit her pay; they just weren't having the right conversations. She "trusted" the company to make the right decisions regarding her pay and they perceived her to be happy with her pay and her career.

In both situations, how the women were *perceived* greatly impacted their compensation and earnings potential. Being a passive player is better than not being a player, but certainly not as good as being an active player.

How do you think you are being perceived?

No matter what your personality type, the most important lesson I can impart is this: **insert yourself in the game.** If you don't play, you can't win. Yes, I am mimicking the lottery commercials, but this sentiment holds true for compensation as well. *If you don't play, you can't win.*

For the rest of this chapter I will discuss each personality powerhouse in detail as it pertains to the compensation process. Up to this point, we have discussed the purpose, mechanics, process, and players. The remainder of this chapter gathers all the information, inserts your personality into the process, and identifies ways to leverage your personality and maximize your pay.

You are ready to learn how to *play* the game and leverage your powerhouse personality.

Step 1: Set the stage

To fully leverage your personality—and maximize your compensation—recap the answers you uncovered about your firm's executive compensation process and its key players. Answer the following questions:

1. What compensation elements are provided by my firm?

2. Which top three compensation elements are most critical to me?

3. What are my firm's characteristics: Is my firm public? Private? Global? In what stage of growth? Revenue size?

4. What is my firm's compensation philosophy? 50th percentile base? 75th percentile base and bonus? Who are our peers?

5. Have I ever been interviewed for my role? Does my job description accurately reflect my responsibilities?

6. Who are the key players in my firm's compensation game?

7. What is each player's degree of influence?

8. What is the relationship between HR and management? Whom do I need to approach?

9. What is my firm's financial performance? What are key financial metrics, stock price, or other financial performance considerations for my firm? What are the potential business challenges and obstacles the firm will be facing?

Keep your answers in mind as we move forward. Because the variables and possible scenarios are almost endless, as we discuss how to leverage your personality and maximize your compensation, I will use three different company scenarios to illustrate possible approaches:

1. A not-for-profit

2. An early stage start-up

3. A mature public company

For each scenario, I will provide potential answers to questions 1 through 9 in the following table. Use these answers as a guideline to determine how the situation might apply to your current organization and situation.

Question	Answer		
	Not-for-profit	Start-Up	Mature Public Co.
1. What compensation elements are provided by my firm?	Base salary and robust benefits	Base, bonus, and equity (highly leveraged). Limited benefits	Base, bonus, potential for equity. Highly competitive benefits
2. Which top 3 elements are most critical to me?	Base and benefits (only two)	Base and equity (only two)	Base, bonus, and benefits
3. Firm characteristics: Is my firm public? Private? Global? Stage of growth? Revenue size?	Large NFP; $50–$100 million operating budget	Pre-IPO; $10m revenues; almost profitable	Global. Public. Fortune 1000

Question	Answer		
	Not-for-profit	**Start-Up**	**Mature Public Co.**
4. What is the firm's compensation philosophy? 50th percentile base? 75th percentile base and bonus? Who are our peers?	Base: 25th–50th percentile of NFP and general industry. Benefits: 50th–75th percentile	Base: 50th–75th. Equity: Based on ownership; more than 75th percentile. Peers: Tech startups	Base: 50th percentile. Bonus and equity: 75th percentile. Benefits: 50th percentile. Peers: Industry competitors, similar in size
5. Have I ever been interviewed for my role? Does my job description accurately reflect my responsibilities?	Maybe	No	Yes
6. Who are the key players in my firm's executive compensation game?	Executive Director, Board, and community	Investors, CEO	Stockholders, Board, and executives

Question	Answer		
	Not-for-profit	Start-Up	Mature Public Co.
7. What is their degree of influence?	Highest: Board	Highest: Investors	Highest: Board and stockholders, CEO (depending on company performance)
8. What is the relationship between HR and management—is HR a critical player?	HR more administrative; implements programs but not key decision maker	HR is outsourced. Few processes. Everything decided as you go along.	HR reports to CEO and part of Board. Very influential.
9. What are key financial metrics, stock price, or other financial performance considerations for my firm? What are the potential business challenges and obstacles the firm will be facing?	Budget of $100 million. Large, stable nonprofit.	No positive cash flow yet—still receiving 2nd and 3rd rounds of financing/funding	EPS and stock price increasing. Low debt levels. Profit margins in line with industry standards. Potential Mergers & Acquisitions as industry consolidates

As discussed in previous chapters, identifying the company's compensation philosophy, which compensation elements are on the table, and who the players are provides invaluable insight regarding how you should play the game. So what does the information in the table tell us? What information do you need to process, understand, and use to improve how you play the game?

In our three scenarios, the information can be further expounded as follows:

Not-for-profit:

1. **Compensation:** Base salary and benefits comprise the most important rewards elements at a not-for-profit.

2. **Players:** HR's role and level of influence will depend on how HR is valued within the organization. In this scenario, the key players with the most influence are the Executive Director, Board of Directors, and the community. HR (in this non-profit) is more of a gatekeeper.

3. **Business Situation:** *Mission critical* is the M.O. at a not-for-profit. When in doubt, reiterate your performance and commitment to the mission. Frame the discussion in terms of achieving the mission. You want to know that the organization values your contributions. (Note: You can retrieve your organization's 990 tax file and learn what pay the Executive Director receives. This information provides you with the "ceiling" in terms of compensation.)

4. **Process:** During your compensation discussion with HR ask about next steps. Focus on process.

Ask what you need to do to move the conversation forward. If you are in a senior role, ensure any next steps include discussions with the Executive Director. This information provides you with the "ceiling" in terms of compensation. Circle back with HR to discuss progress.

Start-up/pre-IPO:

1. **Compensation:** Start-ups may have limited cash and are focused on growth and sales. Therefore, when discussing your contributions, frame your accomplishments in terms of growth and sales. Start-ups may provide bonuses but should provide stock options or restricted stock as well, especially in the early stages. Equity may be less common as the company matures or if the company is in a turnaround situation. In this scenario, base is roughly competitive but the bonus is discretionary and the payouts uncertain. Therefore the focus should be on equity. A lot of equity. Once the company needs more funding, the ownership gets diluted and there is less equity to share. Confirm whether the grant is a one-time grant or an annual grant. An annual grant means you will consistently be awarded equity. If the start-up/IPO is in a turnaround situation, request a retention bonus or larger equity grant to compensate for the risk. In this environment, request more, especially regarding equity. Again, clearly link your contributions to growth and sales.

2. **Players:** In a small start-up, HR may wield little influence over outcome (because the CEO/COO

wants to retain control over compensation deci-sions) but yield a high degree of influence over pro-cess. You need to assess HR's relationship with the CEO/COO. Who is making the compensation decisions—not just communicating them? In this scenario, HR is primarily outsourced, although there is an internal HR contact. The goal should be to meet with the CEO/COO. Communicate what you will deliver in return in terms of growth and sales.

3. **Business Situation:** Typically in a start-up, there are few secrets. You may be aware of what your peers earn. They may know what you earn. That does not mean you should all receive the same compen-sation, but it does provide you with benchmarks.

4. **Process:** Although HR is outsourced, meet with the person responsible for HR first. During the discussion with HR, review next steps. Focus on process. Ask what you need to do to move the con-versation forward. If you are in a senior role, ensure any next steps include discussions with the CEO/COO. If the organization is small, you may be able to set up your own meeting. Ask HR whether you should set up a meeting or whether HR would like to set up a meeting—empowering HR provides you with an ally and helps HR attain more leverage and validity. If the organization does not have any processes or formalities, ask when and how you can expect the compensation proposal to be reviewed and confirmed.

Mature Company:

1. **Compensation:** HR should be extremely sophisti-
cated, with a clear linkage to the business. Process
and protocols have been established and documented. There is a clearly articulated compensation
philosophy along with tested and well-designed
compensation programs. Most mature companies strive for a pay-for-performance environment.
Compensation (and benefits) are clearly linked to
levels within a mature company. Therefore when requesting a promotion, ask to be moved into the next
grade. The next salary grade will have higher bonus
opportunities and better benefits tied to it as well.
For the bonus plan, you may be asked to discuss
your performance against goals. Although you
have limited wiggle room for the financial metrics, continue to sell yourself on the subjective metrics (for example, management by objective)—the
goals with more subjectivity attached. In a mature
organization you will have more limited leverage
regarding equity, so you may need to focus on eligibility and what you can expect once in the plan.
You want to be *in* the plan so you can receive equity. Do your research in terms of what peers at
comparably sized firms and industries offer for the
same role. This data is the easiest to find.

2. **Players:** Your immediate manager is a highly influential player. Because processes are established
in a mature organization, timing is critical. Off-
cycle compensation changes are rare. Meetings
should occur at least six months prior to the fiscal
year-end with your immediate manager. Process is

important, and your manager probably will revert to his or her guidelines and HR regarding your requests.

3. **Business Situation:** Mature companies have clearly established processes and procedures. Powerhouses need to work within the mature company system once hired. However, *prior* to starting, you have greater flexibility and should ask for more. Of everything.

4. **Process:** When meeting with your manager, list accomplishments and achievements as they relate to predetermined performance objectives. For example, if you have achieved exceptional performance but your pay falls low in the salary range, use the performance to your advantage. There is room to move your pay forward in the range, and the movement would be defensible based on your achievements. If you arranged the initial meeting halfway through the year, you should follow up within six weeks. Any appropriate adjustments will not be made until the next performance cycle.

Now we understand the game and the players. Let's play ball.

Step 2: Leverage Your Powerhouse Personality

Like a play, the background, characters, and plot have been developed and now you have an opportunity to influence the end of the story—you are an actor on the stage. Remember the "Choose Your Own Adventure" books in which the reader could select actions and influence the outcome of the story? Just like those books, you are selecting among different actions to influence *your* outcome. Compensation is like an adventure book, and you want to get the most out of your career adventure.

Company leadership (which may include you) uses the information, weighs the data and business objectives, and determines compensation rewards for its employees. Now that you know the game, the decisions can be influenced to positively affect your compensation levels. Using the scenarios I just described, I will now detail how each personality powerhouse can be leveraged to maximize its compensation potential. Ostensibly, each "game" I describe requires a different target audience and compensation approach. Although I discuss possible approaches for each powerhouse, I encourage you to read each powerhouse's recommendations. You may find an approach that works for your situation that isn't discussed in your powerhouse personality playbook.

Personality Powerhouse #1: Assertive

Overall summary: Assertive personality types communicate their opinions and objectives clearly and often. These personalities are more likely to tout their opinions and answers on a regular basis—woven into ongoing conversations. An assertive personality is more likely to assume she is being heard and appropriately compensated *just because she asked for it.*

However, the assertiveness does not always occur at the right times or with the right people.

This is key.

And the fact that she is assertive does not mean that her performance and results are being communicated appropriately. Additionally, assertive personalities still need to ensure they have advocates and allies. Sometimes the assertiveness confuses other people into thinking these women do not need advocates or allies because they are representing themselves. Not true.

Leadership view: Depending on whom the assertive personality told, leadership may or may not remain aware of this person's actions and accomplishments or her expectations regarding compensation. Leadership may expect this personality to offer opinions about how to resolve issues or accomplish tasks, and leadership, in turn, acknowledges receiving the requests (although acknowledgment does not mean approval). Any ensuing compensation increase requests may be acknowledged and considered, *but being assertive does not increase the probability of approval.*

How to leverage this personality: Assertive personalities are, by definition, not shy, and are more likely to showcase the answers to problems on a regular basis. However, whether an assertive personality touts her performance to the right people at the right time is less obvious. To leverage this personality, the assertive powerhouse needs to be assertive at the right time with the right people. She also needs to ensure the results being touted matter to leadership. Assertive personalities need to pay equal tribute to the part of their performance that promotes the company's business strategies, goals, and objectives. For example, "The plan I designed a few months ago resulted in a 10% increase in sales/market share/profits. I believe the reason the plan was successful was because of a combination of factors...[attribute accolades to the team as appropriate]."

Assertive personalities are *not more likely* to ask for compensation increases than the other powerhouses. Assertive personalities are just *more comfortable* asking because they do not fear the social interaction. However, if they do ask, they do not necessarily tie their requests to their performance results and to their strategic importance to the organization. For this powerhouse, asking to be paid and for a certain percentage increase or a specific dollar amount does not always include explaining why the award is warranted. Furthermore, this personality can sometimes ask too frequently.

To effectively leverage their attributes, assertive personalities should not engage in compensation and performance discussions too often, limiting it to perhaps three times annually. If their results truly shine, everyone will be aware of them, although these powerhouses should still reiterate their results when appropriate. Results should be discussed in detail during goal-setting (at the beginning of the performance review), halfway through the year to ensure everyone's perception of the accomplishments are consistent, and two months prior to year end, when compensation, rewards, and recognition decisions are being considered. If this is your personality, ask open-ended questions and refrain from providing the answers—or negotiating against yourself. Instead of offering an amount, wait and listen to what is offered. *Then* ask for more. Do not start by asking for a significant increase because you are more likely to be disappointed with the answer if it is less. And, most likely, because you are an assertive powerhouse, leadership might be expecting you to ask and even to be specific. Therefore, do not play into their preconceived perception. Make them come to you with the answers—do not provide them with the answers.

When engaging the CEO or HR in compensation conversations, explore: what amount of equity should I be expecting? If I deliver X% above the stated goals, what additional base salary increase will be delivered? What level of fundraising, endowments, or budget must be achieved to provide competitive compensation? Sometimes, the company is unable to provide answers, but voicing the questions means your expectations are now more clearly communicated.

Assertive personalities should also develop allies and advocates among the executive ranks. Although this approach is more commonly leveraged by politically savvy powerhouses, it is critical for assertive powerhouses to have friends in the right places as well. Assertive powerhouses can develop advocates and allies with other powerhouses by being outspoken—at the right time—for the other women. For example, tout someone else's performance, give credit where credit is due, or suggest that another woman be given a responsibility because of past performance. The other women will appreciate having an advocate, and they will reciprocate.

> *I once partnered with a financially successful firm where both the Head of HR and the Compensation Manager were women. The Head of HR was a fiercely loyal powerhouse and the Compensation Manager exhibited an assertive personality. During the course of our engagement, we learned that the Head of HR would be leaving the organization—she was pursuing*

*another career opportunity. The organization's
COO also happened to be a woman (confident,
but humble) and was strongly valued by the CEO.
However, despite the Compensation Manager's
assertiveness, she was not being considered for
promotion. She politely and professionally an-
swered questions but did not proactively offer
results-oriented solutions that mattered to leadership. She was a fantastic project manager but
not as strategic a thinker as would be required
for a Head of HR role—she didn't solve the
CEO's problems before they occurred or without
him asking. Being assertive and being successful are not one and the same.*

In all situations: **Communicate your expectations to the
right people. Don't assume your desires will be conveyed
appropriately or at all. You want advocates. If you are too
assertive, you may not have many allies.**

The following examples recap the situation and provides
detailed responses by situation.

Example 1: Not-for-Profit Action Plan

Approach: First meet with HR, with the goal of discussing
your compensation with the Executive Director. Be respectful
of the person's background and influence. Do not talk over
this person—this can easily happen in these situations, especially if HR is not an assertive powerhouse. Discuss your performance and the organization's goals. Ask what HR perceives
competitive pay to be for your role. Ask how HR determines

that number. Remember: do not provide the answer right away. Similarly, you want to make HR your advocate by relating your performance to process and administration. To do this, discuss how your compensation can—and should be—reviewed and revised.

First mirror the organization's values while confirming the organization values your contributions. Then discuss your anticipated pay levels for the role. Because bonuses are not common in not-for-profits, focus on the base salary. Discuss peers and market competitiveness. Discuss your pay positioning within the targeted compensation philosophy. Also thank HR for his/her experience and insight—you may typically thank HR for his/her time, but now you want to emphasize your understanding of HR's role and appreciation of his/her experience.

Example 2: Start-Up/IPO

Approach: First, whenever or however possible, confirm pay levels at comparable organizations or peers. At the beginning of the year, you can ask your manager (or CEO/COO) exactly what performance goals he/she wants to see, how he/she wants to measure them, and what a potential bonus payout might look like. Because you are assertive, you should suggest that a formalized plan benefits everyone and also ensures you are able to meet his/her expectations. You may need to help select the right goals and submit them to the manager for his/her review—but wait to be asked first. Reinforce what matters to him/her and manage his/her expectations.

Without question, you should request restricted stock and stock options. Explain that you want to be paid for delivering exceptional performance and contributing to growth. You only reap rewards if you deliver, and they will reap rewards too. Because you are assertive, you can convey your understanding that investors want sales and growth while reminding the CEO/COO/HR about the inherent risks. Working at a start-up is not as stable as working for a mature company. You want to ensure the grant price is significantly less than expected buy-out or IPO price. Also you will be able to request more options the earlier the company is in its growth and development. If necessary, suggest a schedule based on performance. You can agree to a certain amount of equity in year 1, and then request additional equity after year 2 *if and only if* you achieve prede-termined performance objectives. This clearly links your goals with the founders' goals. Do not be *too* assertive here because you want to ensure the CEO/COO feels in charge.

Example 3: Mature Company

Approach: Meet with your manager as early in the fiscal year as possible. Ask what can be done regarding compensation, what you can expect, and when. If your manager hesitates, reaffirm your commitment and discuss your performance. Confirm the manager knows what you expect in terms of compensation. To show your manager support and become allies, ask your manager to develop a plan for improving your compensation. If he/she falters, you can politely offer to provide him/her with a plan (which you developed prior to this meeting).

The most important thing to do is make your manager your advocate. As an assertive powerhouse, you can do this by touting your manager's performance and abilities at opportune moments (such as in front of his/her manager or other influential people). Be assertive about touting his/her performance and accomplishments. You can significantly leverage this part of your personality. Being other people's spokespersons will win you allies and advocates. Ask your manager when you should follow up.

Personality Powerhouse #2: Confident but Humble

Overall summary: Confident but humble personalities assume that leadership knows they identified an issue, resolved an issue, or impacted the company's bottom line. They may tout their performance sometimes, but less often and in a quiet manner, preferring someone else plays the spokesperson role. These female powerhouses are confident decision-makers and execute all decisions and commitments efficiently and effectively. These personalities *do* link their performance to company results but *do not* try to tout their performance as often—or loudly—as an assertive powerhouse.

Although confident but humble powerhouses communicate their compensation desires, they typical ask for increases they believe are "reasonable" based on their assumptions of what the company can or will do. Therefore, the requests are typically smaller rather than one large increase. Receiving a smaller increase reinforces their confidence—they need to get what they ask for to remain confident. Asking for something that is large and not getting it derails their confidence. In essence, they negotiate against themselves. First, they are less likely to ask for significant increases because they assume they will not receive them. Because these personalities ask for what they *think* the company will provide, they don't ask for enough. Therefore, they negotiate against themselves by establishing a negotiating ceiling that is too low. They may only communicate their compensation desires when they deem it appropriate, and this may not be often enough.

One advantage to these personality powerhouses is that they understand their value and know that they can find another role elsewhere. This understanding should be leveraged.

Leadership view: When asked, confident powerhouses clearly articulate their accomplishments in a manner that links their accomplishments to the company's business. Leadership appreciates this performance linkage but isn't always aware of the role this powerhouse plays in critical business activities because of the "humble" aspect. Confident, but humble personalities prefer other people to extol their praises. They may only communicate their compensation desires when deemed appropriate—and this may not be often enough. Therefore, these powerhouses may not always receive enough credit. Leadership can be unaware of their true role and strategic importance. Additionally, it can appear that leadership takes advantage of this powerhouse's desire to receive what she requests (by requesting only small, "reasonable" increases) and not rock the boat. But if leadership is unaware of her accomplishments, there is no need for them to provide above-market pay.

How to leverage this personality: These female powerhouses are comfortable with their accomplishments and ability to perform. If you are a confident but humble powerhouse, when asking for compensation, you should be more aggressive. If you think you deserve a 5-percent increase, ask for 10 percent. Cite your performance and what you know about peer companies and competitive marketplace pay. Do not assume what the company can or should provide in terms of compensation.

And, if you don't get what you asked for, do not let it unhinge your confidence. It doesn't mean you didn't receive a competitive increase or robust awards.

Finally, you should forge allies with other powerhouses, and encourage others to toot your horn if you are uncomfortable tooting your own horn.

> *I once partnered with a confident but humble CEO working with her Board regarding her compensation package. Both she and the Board knew her compensation could be more competitive relative to market. Because she was new to the role, the Board wanted tangible results before providing more reasonable pay. Once their relationship (between the CEO and Board) solidified, the Board granted her above-market increases until she was brought into a competitive range. The CEO eventually received a more competitive compensation (and benefits) package, but it took time.*

In all situations: **Clearly communicate your expectations—and ask for more at one time. If you are too humble, you will always be slightly below your maximum earning potential.**

Example 1: Not-for-Profit Action Plan

Approach: Similar to the Assertive Powerhouse approach, your first step is to meet with HR. Again, the ultimate goal should be to discuss your compensation with the Executive

Director. During your meeting, use the opportunity to ask what HR believes constitutes competitive pay for your role. Presumably HR will respond with your actual pay level. At this point, dive deeper. Propel the discussion by asking how HR determines that number. Your personality type probably already established a relationship with HR. Therefore, you should have established a professional relationship and foundation where you can comfortably state that you believe the value of your contributions exceed your current pay levels. You may need to provide proof, so research what other nonprofits are paying for comparable roles. You can play to the humble part of your personality by using phrases such as "This responsibility lies with me for not ensuring that my performance and impact to the organization is clearly understood. I would like to take this opportunity to rectify my mistake."

If you determine you are significantly underpaid, separate the discussion into market adjustments and merit increases. The market adjustment brings your pay levels into a competitive range while the merit increase discussion is based on your contributions to the organization. Market adjustments play to the humble part—this seems purely factual and what the company should be delivering in terms of its targeted compensation philosophy. The merit increase plays to the confident part—showcasing your performance and impact on the organization. Request more base because there are no bonuses or equity payouts. If you separate the discussion into market adjustments and merit increases the organization will recognize you understand their financial situation and support the mission. Separating the discussion into both market adjustments and merit increases reinforces your confidence as well. Finally, thank HR for his/her experience and insight.

Example 2: Start-Up/IPO

Approach: In our situation HR is outsourced, so you will meet with your immediate supervisor. At the beginning of the year, you can ask your manager (or CEO/COO) exactly what performance goals he/she wants to see, how he/she wants to measure them, and what a potential bonus payout might look like. Because you are confident, but humble, you should reiterate your belief that you can accomplish these goals. You may need to suggest the right goals and submit them to the manager for his/her review. Reinforce what matters to him/her and manage his/her expectations.

At the appropriate time, remind the CEO/COO/HR about the inherent risks you assumed by taking this role. Once he/she agrees that you assumed risk by working for the company, ask to be compensated for the risk through additional equity. In all situations, ask for more than *you* think is reasonable. **This is the crux of the difference** in this approach for a confident, but humble personality. Do not be *too* conservative in what you request or in what you believe you can (and will) deliver.

Example 3: Mature Company

Approach: When meeting with your manager, discuss your concerns and request increases that exceed *your* perception of reasonableness. Allow negotiating room but do not be intimidated if you're told that there are policies and procedures. Do not let the mature company sway your confidence and convey the perception that it cannot deliver. Ask for larger base salary increases, a greater bonus payout, and additional equity than you think you deserve. Confirm that your manager knows what you expect in terms of compensation.

In mature companies, because processes have already been established. HR can always rely on the processes in place (and need for internal equity) to refuse your requests. Confident powerhouses might understand this and work too hard to stay within the system once hired. Ask for more. There is room.

Because you deliver on your performance, your manager should be your advocate. You need to actually *confirm* this. Don't assume your manager actually represents what you think should be represented. Be specific. Ask your manager what needs to be done to receive a raise. By asking your manager to detail what he/she believes is required, you are making your problem *his/her* problem. This signifies an unspoken contract or commitment that if you deliver, you will be paid.

Personality Powerhouse #3: Politically Savvy

Overall summary: Politically savvy women mastermind networks and alliances. They know how to negotiate the water cooler talk, culture, and power chain at the office. As a result, they believe others will take care of them and do the talking for them when it comes to compensation. Or they believe they can plant the seed and it will be communicated to the right person. And because they believe someone is their advocate, they *assume* that person is compensating or rewarding or recognizing them appropriately. As you now understand, these assumptions limit their successes.

Leadership view: Leadership leverages politically savvy female powerhouses to promote the culture, reinforce communication and key messages, and be a "face" for the company—promoting goodwill, focus on women and women's objectives, and work-life balance. Because politically savvy women assume they are being protected or promoted, leadership does not have to pay them excessively if everyone is on the same page. If one of this powerhouse's advocates disagrees, then leadership will review the package.

How to leverage this personality: Become as informed as possible regarding the process and then speak privately with your advocates. Politically savvy women may think they are being compensated well if they aren't part of the actual compensation process—in other words, they aren't privy to how they are being paid relative to the firm's target market and targeted compensation philosophy. Be specific about your performance and your desired compensation goals. Let your network fight for you but don't assume they know how much you want. Confirm your entire network (all your senior advocates) knows your expectations so they can deliver. And, confirm your network consists of the real decision-makers regarding compensation. If not, earn their support.

At my very first client meeting, I learned about perception (though all the lessons were not entirely clear at first). The client, a global chemical company, was represented by the CEO and VP of HR. Our team included the partner, consultant, and me (the analyst). For me, it was supposed to be a learning experience. And it was. The CEO did all the talking during the meeting. The VP of HR brought us drinks. At first, I thought the VP of HR was weak. She didn't say anything. But after two more years working with this client (when a new CEO was brought on), I realized she was very, very smart. And politically savvy. New CEOs typically hire new senior

management teams. But this VP of HR main-
tained her role within the organization. She had
aligned herself appropriately. She was paid well
and kept her job when the new CEO started. She
was loyal when she needed to be and distanced
herself when she needed to stay at arm's length.
She was incredibly politically savvy.

In all situations: **Work your networks and advocates. Convey your compensation desires clearly and explicitly.**

Example 1: Not-for-Profit Action Plan

Approach: If you have been working your networks, you should be on friendly terms with HR and the Executive Director. If not, start now. Empower HR by expressing a keen interest in the person, what he/she does, and how he/she does it.

After focusing on your commitment to the mission, discuss your anticipated pay levels for the role. Ask HR how he/she thinks you should approach compensation and a pay raise. Enlist HR's help. You can also plant a number in HR's head, such as 5 percent, because that would bring you into the competitive range. Explain that you understand HR works diligently to promote a competitive compensation philosophy. Persuasive conversation—the kind that encourages the other person to think your argument is a sound argument—is your best tool to employ. You want to make your problem HR's problem, and your powerhouse personality has the skills to put the monkey on their back.

If you determine you are significantly underpaid, separate the discussion into market adjustments and merit increases. The market adjustment brings your pay levels into competitive range while the merit increase discussion is based on your contributions to the organization. Empathize with HR's plight—trying to deliver a competitive compensation program while working within strict financial parameters. Try to get HR to empathize with you—wanting to be paid competitively for achieving the organization's mission. Thank HR for his/her experience and insight. You can even go so far as to ask HR how you can help him/her be successful.

Example 2: Start-Up/IPO

Approach: Advocacy is the name of the game at a start-up, and this is your bailiwick. You want the CEO and COO to be your advocates. Because you are politically savvy, you may already be on friendly terms. You need to use your powers of persuasion to ensure they are your advocates as well. If you are in a senior role, and have access to investors, you want to ensure their advocacy as well.

To ensure the CEO/COO supports your professional success, clearly link your contributions to CEO and CEO performance as well as growth and sales. The CEO and COO also want to be successful and receive payouts. If you are politically savvy you understand the importance of empathy and the results that empathizing with others produces. Empathize with the CEO/COO. Empathize with his/her passion for the company, desire to succeed, and need for growth. This will improve your leverage. When asking for base salary increases and equity, communicate your commitment to the company's success.

At the beginning of the year, you can ask your manager (or CEO/COO) exactly what performance goals he/she wants to see, how he/she wants to measure them, and what a potential bonus payout might look like. Because you are politically savvy, you can do this in a way that matters to him/her while managing his/her expectations (this is called "managing up").

After being hired, grow and work your networks. Become friendly with different executives, Board members, and investors. Ensure everyone understands that you (and your performance) are critical to the company's financial success. And, if at all possible (depending on your level), insert yourself into the compensation process if you are privy to that information. If not, develop a plan for more actively inserting yourself into the process.

Example 3: Mature Company

Approach: Because you are well-networked, you may know how other groups or departments are managed. Leverage this information. Your manager will confer with HR, but also with other managers. The more you know, the better. For example, if you know that other people have received higher raises, say so. Don't name names or begrudge the other person, just ask for the same treatment.

For the bonus plan, sell yourself on the subjective metrics—the goals with more subjectivity attached. You are good at selling yourself. Use this tool.

Show your manager you want him/her to be successful as well. Link your performance to your manager's performance. If your manager is taking care of himself/herself, he/she will then want to take care of you. Again, you are skilled at making others *want* to promote you. Leverage this skill—just confirm that leadership understands your expectations.

The most important action is to make your manager your advocate. You should understand what motivates your manager. Play on that motivation. If your manager needs certain results to "look good," focus on how your contributions improve those results.

Personality Powerhouse #4: Fiercely Loyal

Overall summary: As the name conveys, these personalities— extremely loyal and dedicated powerhouses—breathe the company culture and are an important asset to leadership. Many other women in the firm consider fiercely loyal powerhouses to be role models because of their tenure and dedication and, therefore, having appeared to achieve work-life balance. Fiercely loyal powerhouses are well liked and believe they are—or will be—rewarded appropriately. Their most important trait: their belief in the company and other people. They have faith in the world. They want and need other people or institutions to meet their expectations. These powerhouses are trusting, but if that trust is violated, it is difficult to regain. Fiercely loyal powerhouses are high performers that are recognized and rewarded at an average pace. They receive good increases and bonuses but, generally, not *stellar* increases and bonuses. When any employee stays with a company for several years (through economic booms and lulls), market pay increases tend to outpace company pay increases. Therefore, long-term employees can have salaries that lag behind the market. Companies are not purposely undercompensating these powerhouses in this situation; it is the nature of the beast. The market might experience a boom of 8 percent salary increases for one year while employees receive pay increases at 4 percent (for example, new-hire salary offers outpace pay raises at a company, so current employee salaries will lag behind a new hire's salary). On the flip side, because these women do not actively (and loudly) tout their performance, they aren't aggressively managing their career progression and/or compensation.

Leadership View: Leadership recognizes and values this powerhouse's loyalty. By delivering average (or slightly above average) increases and bonuses, leadership believes it is rewarding that loyalty without having to pay too much. Leadership may also reward the loyalty with intangible benefits such as a lot of work-balance flexibility, increased responsibilities (not necessarily promotions), or other career development opportunities.

How to leverage this personality: Fiercely loyal powerhouses need to trust; trusting comprises the fabric of their personality and foundation for their relationships with people and/or companies. Although they act on this trust, they do not always communicate this expectation. By sharing the simple fact that they trust their manager to "do the right thing," they are almost forcing other people to espouse their same values. When other people realize the amount of trust being placed in them, they will be more likely to deliver.

After capitalizing on their method of relationship-building (trusting other people), these female powerhouses need to clearly articulate their expectations—exactly how much raise they are expecting and when—and their disappointment at learning that their loyalty and performance are not valued by the company, or at least not as much as a new hire. Leverage this point. **Expressly acknowledge that the company no longer values you.** This is the most important leverage in a fiercely loyal powerhouse's arsenal. This is not how the company wants to be perceived, because this means the trust is lost and therefore the relationship is in jeopardy. The company will respond that it *does* value the powerhouse, but simply pointing to the current compensation discrepancies will dispel that argument.

At the same time, fiercely loyal powerhouses need to be willing to walk away. Focusing on self-confidence can improve this female powerhouse's negotiating strategies. If leadership believes these female powerhouses are a flight risk, they will provide more competitive compensation, rewards, and opportunities. There is a significant opportunity cost with losing these fiercely loyal women—other employees highly value these female powerhouses. Their departure signals a potential issue with the company and its treatment of employees. Use this point to your advantage.

> *Almost every time I discuss women and pay at conferences, half the room thinks they are the fiercely loyal type. This tends to have less to do with tenure and more to do with feeling (or wanting) the company to "do the right thing." Companies aren't necessarily doing the wrong thing. Again, most aren't. This is about taking a more active role in the process to get more pay than you might have otherwise. Fiercely loyal powerhouses feel uncertain about taking this active role.*

In all situations: **Unfortunately, loyalty is not always rewarded. You have to clearly state your understanding that you are not being valued in a manner consistent with the**

company's compensation philosophy or performance expectations, or in a manner consistent with what you have
delivered.

Example 1: Not-for-Profit Action Plan

Approach: If you aren't already friendly with HR, become
friendly. HR will most likely empathize with your plight because your pay levels are most likely on the low end of the
competitive range. Ask HR how he/she thinks you should approach compensation and a pay raise. Enlist HR's help. At the
same time, you will need to be more specific about what you
want or what you are willing to accept.

Focus on your relationship with HR. Relationship-
building—and trust—are the cornerstone of this powerhouse.
Empathize with HR's plight: trying to deliver a competitive
compensation program while working within strict financial
parameters. Try to get HR to empathize with you—wanting to
be paid competitively for achieving the organization's mission.

**The difference at a nonprofit for fiercely loyal power-
houses:** Communicate with HR what you know about the
marketplace and perhaps about internal metrics as well. If you
know that peers earn more than you, despite your stellar performance, then it is time to politely tattle. Your powerhouse personality can use this information to make HR feel as though
the relationship—and sense of trust—has been violated.

Reiterate your own performance and goal achievement.
This is not something fiercely loyal types typically do. If you
are a high performer, the organization needs you. If the organization believes you may leave, they will be more likely to approve your increase. **You need to appear dissatisfied to the**

point of being willing to break up with the company and resign.

Because you relied on HR in the past to do the right thing, assume more control of the process now. Ask what you can expect and when. If you are in a senior role, ensure any next steps include discussions with the executive director. Inquire as to how you can help HR to succeed in this goal—do not let the momentum subside.

Example 2: Start-Up/IPO

Approach: Before meeting with your supervisor or the person responsible for HR, do your research. What do you want? What are you willing to accept? What might make you walk away? Fiercely loyal powerhouses can be easily swayed if the focus is switched to the relationship rather than the outcomes. Therefore you need to go in prepared. When asking for compensation increases, communicate your commitment to the company's success. Communicate what you will deliver in terms of growth and sales. **This is the crux of the difference** in this approach for the fiercely loyal powerhouse. You need to tout your own performance—strongly—and *believe* what you are saying. **Do not assume you will be treated fairly.** In a start-up, where there are no rules, there is no fair play either.

Because you are fiercely loyal, you should reinforce your loyalty (verbally anyway) and use that to your advantage. Replacing employees is expensive—they don't want the added cost. Furthermore, you can help engage other employees. Reinforce what matters to them and manage their expectations.

The best way to improve your leverage (if you have to) is appear be a flight risk and/or openly discuss the fact that you are aware of what other people earn. Just being willing to walk improves your self-confidence and negotiating power. In a small environment, where there are no secrets, leadership does not want dissension. Remember to use your ability to trust as a competitive advantage. Tell HR/the CEO you trust them to be developing and implementing fair compensation practices because that supports the type of culture they are trying to create. Reiterate that you want to be an integral part of that type of culture and leadership. If at any point during the conversation you feel as though you are being swayed or played, then take a break. Ask to get some water or use the restroom. Regroup and then return ready to move forward.

And, if leadership does not follow through, then most likely things won't change until there is different leadership in place. You need to decide if you can wait.

Example 3: Mature Company

Approach: Fiercely loyal powerhouses focus on the messages received regarding the established processes and procedures. These messages are used to sway the fiercely loyal powerhouse from requesting *more*. Therefore, if you are a fiercely loyal powerhouse, use the process to your advantage. Revisit the compensation philosophy and structure and where the company says you should be based paid on your performance and experience.

You need your manager to be your advocate. Show your manager you want him/her to be successful as well. Link your performance to your manager's performance. If your manager is taking care of himself/herself, he/she will then want to take care of you. You may need to have an honest conversation and convey that you realize you haven't been valued, despite your performance and loyalty. By acknowledging your recognition of the situation, your manager will be more concerned you might leave and more likely to act.

The most important action is to inform your manager in a way that transforms him/her into your advocate. **Also, if your manager needs you to be successful *and* perceives you as a flight risk, you will be more likely to get what you desire.**

Conclusion

Each powerhouse's playbook given in this chapter provided tips for maximizing the compensation opportunities available to you. Remember: learn the game, learn the players, and then leverage your role in the game. Gather as much information as possible before making your move. And play to your strengths. That is the best way to improve how you are perceived, and, ultimately, how high your compensation is.

The tips provided depend on each powerhouse personality's strengths. Of course, an assertive powerhouse can employ the confident, but humble playbook, but the degree—and probability—of success will be directly related to the powerhouse's ability to "sell" the play. Ultimately, you want to improve how you are perceived in order to improve your compensation awards.

Perception = reality.

Always.

CHAPTER 7

Special Situations: How to Handle a Blitz

Sometimes during a powerhouse's career her company will request that employees assume a high level of risk. The unexpected happens. The company makes a move you didn't anticipate.

During these situations, potential termination looms in the distance. Perhaps the company is merging, acquiring another firm, or divesting a business. Perhaps the company is undergoing a massive restructuring, realigning roles and eliminating positions. Powerhouses might be asked to lead the transition or leave the current organization with the divestiture and work for the new company. Whenever you are asked to assume new, different, additional, or high-risk responsibilities, discuss compensation.

Always.

First, you must decide whether you can reasonably accept the proposed role and requirements. If you decide to decline the assignment, you should discuss the terms for your termination, including severance.

Prior to meeting with your boss, determine what you *want* to have and what you *need* to have for the situation to be acceptable. Remember, numerous compensation and benefits elements are in play—base, bonus, equity, relocation, etc. If you are nearing retirement, you could ask for an early retirement package as well.

But you need to *ask*. Here's how.

Let's assume the company decided to divest a significant portion of the business. You have been asked to transition to the new company. Your choices: **accept** the new position with the new firm or **decline** and request a severance package. In this scenario, I am assuming the benefits are comparable. Now let's see how each powerhouse chooses to accept or decline.

Assertive Powerhouse

Accept

Say, "This business opportunity is the right strategic move for our organization and I am glad to be part of it. It is a necessary part of business and in the best interests of our stakeholders." Transitioning to a new firm presents itself with risks, so you agree to successfully lead the transition in return for the following compensation in return:

◑ Base increase of 6 to 10 percent (you decide how much you feel comfortable requesting) because you do not know when the new company will incorporate you into their rewards program and you do not want your compensation to be lagging.

◑ A guaranteed bonus of $X to ensure a smooth transition. This is due to the concern that the new company may not keep your role. This should be paid prior to your becoming an employee of the new company.

◑ A letter from the new company discussing the terms of the employment, the position, and the compensation. If the company is public, you will want an equity grant (upon hire) as well as the guaranteed bonus for the first year.

Decline

Say, "This business opportunity is the right strategic move for the company. It is a necessary part of business and in the best interests of our stakeholders. However, I selected this company because of its culture and leadership, and I do not feel the new entity is a good fit and have decided to pursue other opportunities." Still, you *can* successfully complete the divestiture operations within the desired timeframe. To help transition the divestiture, you could require the following:

◑ A retention bonus of $X (select an amount at least between 10 and 20 percent of your base salary) to "close" the current operations.

- ⟲ A severance package equal to your most recent base salary and bonus, plus health and welfare benefit coverage.

- ⟲ A carefully determined end date. If possible, choose an end date *after* your next bonus payout to ensure the bonus payouts are included in any benefits/retirement calculations. If this isn't possible, consider your benefits—you may need to negotiate a special arrangement to ensure the highest valuation possible is attributed to these programs.

- ⟲ Written references prior to your end date.

Confident, but Humble Powerhouse

Accept

Say, "This is an exciting business opportunity and I can absolutely transition this divestiture, including all operations and systems." Reiterate an appreciation for their confidence in your leadership to lead this divestiture. Explain that you recognize that you can contribute greatly to the new company. To ensure a smooth transition and be rewarded for your efforts, request the following:

- ⟲ A base increase of 6 to 10 percent (you decide how much you feel comfortable requesting) because you do not know when the new company will incorporate you into their rewards program and you do not want your compensation to be lagging.

- ⟲ A guaranteed bonus of $X to ensure a smooth transition. This is due to the concern that the new company may not keep your role. This should be paid prior to your becoming an employee of the new company.

ↄ A letter from the new company discussing the terms of your employment, your position, and your compensation. If the company is public, you should request an equity grant as well as a guaranteed bonus for the first year.

Decline

Say, "I realize this is an exciting business opportunity for the firm and I have given this considerable thought. Unfortunately, it is not in my career goals to work for the new company." Therefore, you can complete the transition but do not want to work at the new company. Because of your contributions to this firm, and based on the company's policies and practices, you should request the following:

ↄ A retention bonus of $X (select an amount between 10 and 20 percent of your base salary) to "close" the current operations.

ↄ A severance package equal to your most recent base salary and bonus, plus health and welfare benefit coverage.

ↄ Final payouts of all outstanding compensation programs—such as any vested equity. You can ask for any unvested equity to be vested immediately.

ↄ A carefully determined final end date. If possible, choose an end date *after* your next bonus payout to ensure the bonus payouts are included in any benefits/retirement calculations. If this isn't possible, consider your benefits—you may need to negotiate a special arrangement to ensure the highest valuation possible is attributed to these programs.

◯ Written references prior to your end date.

Politically Savvy Powerhouse

Accept

Say, "Thank you for thinking of me for this critical role." It affords you a good deal of leadership experience in a high-risk environment. Explain that you also appreciate the recognition that you can be successful at the new company in this particular role and are looking forward to the challenge and to meeting their leadership. Closing successfully is critical for both companies involved, and you can successfully transition the operations with minimal to no business disruptions. In order to effectively close the operations, maintain client satisfaction, and lead employees during this difficult time, you would like to discuss the compensation package. Although you are confident the company has already prepared a competitive package, you would like to confirm both of your expectations are being met. To be clear, you want:

◯ A base increase of 6 to 10 percent (you decide how much you feel comfortable requesting) because you do not know when the new company will incorporate you into their rewards program and you do not want your compensation to be lagging.

🜋 A guaranteed bonus of $X to ensure a smooth transition. This is due to the concern that the new company may not keep your role. This should be paid prior to your becoming an employee of the new company.

🜋 A letter from the new company discussing the terms of the employment, the position, and the compensation. If the company is public, you will want an equity grant (upon hire) as well as the guaranteed bonus for the first year.

Decline

Say, "Thank you for thinking of me for this critical role. Although I greatly appreciate the efforts made to secure me a role in this new organization, I believe it is in my best interests to pursue other opportunities after the closing takes place. Based on our relationship, I believe this is something you can understand." You are still committed to closing the operations successfully, and you can transition the operations with minimal to no business disruptions. In order to effectively close the operations, maintain client satisfaction, and lead employees during this difficult time, you would like to discuss the compensation package. Although you are sure they have already prepared a competitive package, you would like to confirm both of your expectations are being met. To be clear, you want:

🜋 A retention bonus of $X (select an amount between 10 and 20 percent of your base salary) to "close" the current operations.

- A severance package equal to your most recent base salary and bonus, plus health and welfare benefit coverage.

- Final payouts of all outstanding compensation programs such as any vested equity. You can ask for any unvested equity to be vested immediately.

- A carefully determined final end date. If possible, choose an end date *after* your next bonus payout to ensure the bonus payouts are included in any benefits/retirement calculations. If this isn't possible, consider your benefits—you may need to negotiate a special arrangement to ensure the highest valuation possible is attributed to these programs.

- Written references prior to your end date.

Fiercely Loyal Powerhouse

Accept

Say, "Thank you for believing that I can contribute successfully to this new organization. I have always been dedicated to this company and its strategic objectives. I appreciate the consideration given to my performance and achievements and want to make the new entity a success." Although you are confident the company has already prepared a competitive package, you would like to confirm both of your expectations are being met. Your expectations are:

- A base increase of 6 to 10 percent (you decide how much you feel comfortable requesting) because you do not know when the new company will incorporate you into their rewards program and you do not want your compensation to be lagging.

◑ A guaranteed bonus of $X to ensure a smooth transition. This is due to the concern that the new company may not keep your role. This should be paid prior to your becoming an employee of the new company.

◑ A letter from the new company discussing the terms of the employment, the position, and the compensation. If the company is public, you will want an equity grant (upon hire) as well as the guaranteed bonus for the first year.

Decline

Say, "Thank you for believing that I can contribute successfully to this new organization. After working together with you and other terrific people for so long, it is difficult for me to imagine working anywhere else. However, I do not believe the new organization is the right place for me at this point in my career. I am committed to helping the company transition, though, and want to see the venture be successful." Although you are sure they have already prepared a competitive package, you would like to confirm both of your expectations are being met. Your expectations are:

◑ A retention bonus of $X (select an amount between 10 and 20 percent of your base salary) to "close" the current operations.

- ◐ A severance package equal to your most recent base salary and bonus, plus health and welfare benefit coverage.

- ◐ Final payouts of all outstanding compensation programs such as any vested equity. You can ask for any unvested equity to be vested immediately.

- ◐ A carefully determined end date. If possible, choose an end date *after* your next bonus payout to ensure the bonus payouts are included in any benefits/retirement calculations. If this isn't possible, consider your benefits—you may need to negotiate a special arrangement to ensure the highest valuation possible is attributed to these programs.

- ◐ Written references prior to your end date.

Conclusion

Each powerhouse personality achieves significant performance results. Staying true to your personality significantly increases your chances of achieving your compensation goals. You can most effectively "sell" your desires in your natural state. Trying to be something you aren't will weaken your position—the company won't believe the message. Leveraging the right aspects of each powerhouse personality improves how you are perceived, and ultimately, how you are compensated.

You may determine that the proposed course of action for one personality type better suits your needs in this situation, even if you are generally a different personality type. The suggestions I've given stay true to the main threads of each personality but can—and should—be tailored and altered as needed.

Finally, ask for the agreement to be written and signed by the company.

Always.

CHAPTER 8

Ignore the Gender Gap

If you Google the words "gender pay gap," the first page highlights links to discussing (a) the reasons behind the gap, (b) why the gap is a myth, and (c) how to close the gap. Googling "gender pay gap" produces the same facts, myths, and legends as Googling the Loch Ness Monster or Bigfoot. Separating the myth from reality can cause a migraine.

On the surface, it seems as though whether or not a gender gap exists should be a yes-or-no question. Politicians, women's advocacy groups, and the media promote the existence of a gender gap for different purposes. Political reasons, unfortunately, seem less altruistic: ostensibly to promote the equitable treatment of women in the workforce, but really to gain the female vote. Women's advocacy groups focus on the *perceived* root cause: discrimination. The media reports and recounts issues of gender gap violations to incite and prolong the debate, fuel the fire, and increase coverage and viewership.

So what is the gender gap? Simply stated, the gender gap comprises women's earnings, on average, expressed as a percentage of male earnings. For example, most studies report that women (on average) earn 80 percent of what men earn, and therefore conclude that a gender gap exists. The Bureau of Labor Statistics reports that currently women earn approximately 81 to 82 cents on the dollar of their male counterparts.[1] When the Bureau of Labor Statistics compares the earnings of women to men, the data is aggregated based on age. Compensation earned by women between the ages of 25 and 34 are compared to compensation earned by men in the same age group. When women earn less than men, the gender-gap bell is rung. *Ding Ding Ding!*

Numerous studies exist *proving* the gender gap actually exists. However, most academics agree the data is seriously flawed, or at the very least, should be thoroughly questioned and examined. First, the data is compiled in the aggregate and only segregated based on age, not based on company or position. If you compare a 34-year-old female accountant to a 34-year-old male ophthalmologist, the female accountant is going to earn less.

That does not mean there is a gender gap.

Other academics underscore that any actual wage discrepancies are due to personal choices, such as leaving the workforce to raise children or choosing lower-paying jobs in exchange for work/life balance. In other words, comparing women between the ages of 35 and 44 to men between the ages of 35 and 44 will produce a gender gap because many women took a leave of absence, stalling both their careers and compensation progression. Therefore, their careers and compensation did not progress at the same rate. In other words, it isn't a fair comparison.

That does not mean there is a gender gap.

For various reasons, men log longer hours than women. The Department of Labor conducted the American Time Use Survey and, based on this survey, the Bureau of Labor Statistics reported that men worked an average of 9 percent more hours than women in 2012.[2] At the executive level, this could result in more rapid promotions or higher bonuses.

That does not mean there is a gender gap.

Several articles highlights that men are more apt to choose jobs that require intense physical labor or more dangerous conditions. The top 10 most dangerous jobs—according to the Bureau of Labor Statistics[3]—are male-dominated, and those dangerous working conditions warrant more pay.

That does not mean there is a gender gap.

Clearly, the data can—and is—manipulated to prove a particular point of view. The main issue boils down to one of discrimination. The concern any individual should have is not in the aggregate, but singularly pointed at a specific situation. A gender gap exists *if* a particular company purposely compensates women less than their male counterparts, **for the same role/responsibilities and the same level of performance**.

Again, when deciding whether a gender gap exists, the comparison needs to be between people performing the *same* role for the *same* company. Otherwise, it isn't a fair comparison. In other words, if both a male and female oversee a $1 billion division for a $3 billion manufacturing company, and both people have the same experience, performance, and impact on the organization, *and* the women is paid less, then yes, there *is* a gender gap.

The studies generally agree on one point: A pay gap may be less likely to exist among lower-level roles, but more likely to magnify among higher-level roles. A 2013 study from PayScale concluded that as women progress in their careers, compensation for men starts to outpace those of women.[4] This study suggests the gap promulgates at the executive level. But that does not mean the gap is due to discrimination. It could be due to pursuing roles that command less compensation, due to underperforming relative to male peers, or due to playing the compensation game less well.

Point #1: Women Need to Perceive Higher Levels of Compensation as Fair

The gap, if there is one, I believe manifests primarily because women aren't asking for enough. In my experience, companies and men do not *purposely* or *consciously* pay women less. In fact, I believe companies pay what is *perceived* as fair and competitive.

If you are *one* female executive in charge of *one* function or operation at a company, and your male peers, in charge of different functions or operations, receive more compensation, that does not mean there is a gender gap. If a company pays one man more than one woman at the executive level, that does not automatically imply that a gender gap exists. It just means these particular men earn more money. And it does *not* mean their female peers are being underpaid. This particular woman might be earning a very pretty penny for the role she is performing.

I have sat in many Boardrooms, listened to many compensation discussions, and observed the decision-making process. In most cases, the leaders (typically men) award what is perceived to be competitive and fair, in line with the company's compensation philosophy and based on individual performance. No one is overtly trying to undermine the women.

Of course, that does not mean female powerhouses shouldn't try to earn more. Women can—and should—earn as much as possible.

At the same time, I would be remiss if I professed never witnessing instances of gender biases. I absolutely did. And, as part of good governance and due diligence, at those companies my firm and I recommended ways to improve pay levels and remove the discrepancies. Surprisingly, some firms aren't aware of the potential issues. Sometimes it has to be identified by an outside source.

Point #2: Women Are Not Underpaid, They Are Just Not Paid as Competitively as Possible

In my experience, in companies that articulate a sound compensation philosophy and establish programs supporting this philosophy, women are paid in the competitive range, but not as competitively as possible. It is also my experience that women tend to suffer greater pay disparities in companies and organizations where there is no articulated philosophy, and where pay is approached on an ad hoc basis. For these companies, women need to diligently research their market value and clearly communicate their expectations; knowledge is power, and assertiveness helps. These employers apply the "back of the envelope" approach to pay—it is haphazard at best without any solid foundation. These companies can't track what they are doing or don't take the time to ensure internal equity and external competitiveness. My second point pertains to those companies that clearly establish guiding principles for their compensation program.

Back to the beginning (of this book), companies establish compensation philosophies and manage pay according to these philosophies. There is some latitude within each philosophy for administering pay. Competitive pay is not one data point but a range of data points. There is also a range of competitiveness—a reasonable range. Any point within this range would be considered competitive both internally and externally. You want to be in the high end of the range.

The following table illustrates this point.

Incumbent	Role	Base Salary	Competitive Range	Position in Range
Sally Smith	Chief Marketing Officer	$250k	$240–$325k	Low End
John Doe	Chief Finance Officer	$300k	$225–$310k	High End

In this fictitious example, both incumbents are paid competitively. Both executives receive compensation that achieves the company's stated compensation philosophy. However, the man's earnings are *more* competitive than the woman's. Although a gender gap does not exist here, the woman could earn higher levels of compensation relative to the market data and stated positioning.

This is the game women need to learn and to play:

1. Understand how the company collects and uses data.

2. Leverage your personality—improve your perception.

3. Get paid for the value of your contributions with your knowledge of #1 and #2.

It bears repeating: Being underpaid—or paid less—does not mean there is a gender gap. In other words, being underpaid—or paid less—does not automatically imply discrimination. Women can exercise more control over their compensation than they realize. Women just need to gain control by inserting themselves in the process and playing the game effectively.

At the executive level, a gender gap is harder to prove. There isn't an overabundance of firms with multiple, comparable executive roles that employ both men and women with the same responsibility, background, experience, and performance. And many of the firms I advised paid their senior female executives handsomely.

We were engaged by a global media/telecommunications firm to help them evaluate their global leveling. They had 75 to 100 executive positions across different divisions, with different definitions (or levels of responsibility) attached to each title. Each division had a different system. Through our interviews and research, we had the pleasure of meeting with one of the top executives, a woman. She oversaw a smaller segment of the business by revenue but its strategic impact was huge—her business was the firm's future. Therefore she demanded (and received) significant compensation relative to her peers. Despite the smaller P&L she oversaw, she understood the value of her business relative to the company as a whole, and she leveraged that value into competitive compensation. More impressive, most of the other senior executives were men. She was one of a few women in the firm and she was paid well.

Do you believe in Bigfoot?

The more important question is, do *you* believe a gender gap exists? And, if so, is your perception undermining your self-confidence and limiting your earnings potential? If you believe a gender gap exists, and further believe you are being targeted by it, you won't be able to fully leverage your opportunities and maximize your compensation. The fears about the gender gap will inhibit your confidence and ability to appropriately tout your performance and achieve financial success. Your inhibitions will dampen your negotiating abilities and bargaining power, so women need to first shed their inhibitions and anything weakening their confidence.

Easier said than done? Sometimes. But you can do it.

Before you develop a productive strategy for playing the game and leveraging your personality, renew your energy. Think like an athlete. Refocus. Shed the losses. Shed the guilt. Shed the past. Leave any lingering doubts or suspicions behind. Forget about how you have been "wronged," and move forward. That is the only way to leverage your personality and earn more money. Companies take advantage of weakness—and believing in a gender gap is a weakness.

> *On numerous occasions, I encountered women capped professionally by their grudges. These women wore their grudges openly. They constantly perceived colleagues or leaders as viable threats rather than allies. The amount of energy devoted to ensuring they weren't outshined by others was inevitably perceived negatively by those in a position to dole out awards, promotions, and accolades. These women, although exceptional at their roles, failed to conquer the most senior executive ranks or be paid appropriately. Being a truly effective leader requires self-awareness, collaboration, business acumen, and effective decision-making. The grudge becomes a shield blocking collaboration and, therefore, effective leadership.*

I am suggesting you reaffirm your confidence, develop a strategy, and then proceed. To be successful in this endeavor, women need to maintain calmness, a strong core, and the ability to disengage from the emotional barriers that weigh us down. Assuming the world is against us defeats our purpose and minimizes our chances of success. This larger-than-life chip on the shoulder is blatantly visible, and it does not encourage career success. The chip does not encourage others to offer us opportunities, recognize our value, and compensate us appropriately.

> *I once partnered with a female powerhouse who lugged a chip on her shoulder. She constantly reminded others of her importance, how the firm didn't value her or her work enough, and how other employees and peers should value her more. As a result of this chip, she was never rewarded with more responsibility or the recognition she craved. And she was not the role model she could have been to other female employees. The chip effectively blocked her chances of maximizing her professional successes.*

Jim Loehr, a world-renowned performance psychologist, author of the ground-breaking book *The Only Way to Win* and co-author of the national best-seller *The Power of Full Engagements*, trained many of today's recognized business leaders. According to press releases and his company's Website (*www.hpinstitute.com*), Dr. Loehr maintains that the most important factor in achieving a successful professional and personal life is the strength of one's character. Translated into my terms: *whichever powerhouse personality dominates, make it your center.*

Dr. Loehr once observed that tennis players renew their energy between points by turning away from the net and refocusing. If you find yourself staring at the net but unable to get the ball over, turn away and renew your energy. Then start again. Get ready to serve an ace. Don't attempt the second serve until you are ready. Similarly, walking through the day assuming there is a gender gap to leap will only cause a double fault. So if you need to, walk away from the net. Before leveraging your personality, fortify your self-confidence. Without confidence, achieving your own definition of success becomes unattainable. Being confident means being certain that your chosen course of action is the *best* or most *effective*. If you have little or weak self-confidence, you will constantly question your choices, career path, or approach to playing the game. Without self-confidence, you can't succeed.

Over and over again, I am floored by how seemingly amazing, high-performing, and accomplished women lack confidence, or at least harbor inner demons that damage their self-esteem. Subtle reasons typically linger under the surface. Personal setbacks rank as the most common antagonist of self-confidence.

I once partnered with a senior powerhouse within the financial services industry. This woman leapt over every corporate ladder, constantly achieving new heights and accomplishments. However, at one organization, a separation occurred due to a business restructuring. Despite the fact the situation was not indicative of her performance, her confidence crumbled. Her past accomplishments faded and it took time and lots of reassurance to rebuild her psyche.

To rebuild—or just fortify—your self-confidence, take care of you. Don't neglect your personal, physical, and emotional needs. Here are four ways you can bolster your self-confidence.

1. Healthy Mind, Healthy Body

Find mental balance through exercise, a nutritionally balanced diet, and sleep. Studies upon studies support the theory that being physically and mentally healthy improves self-confidence. If you feel good about yourself physically, you feel good mentally. And positive mental health directly correlates to positive self-confidence. Furthermore, exercise accelerates your endorphins—the feel-good neurotransmitters. Exercise acts like an organic drug that minimizes stress, improves your overall mood, boosts self-confidence, and lowers symptoms associated with anxiety and depression.

Dr. John Grohol, PsyD, studies the connection between physical and mental health. On his Website, world of psychology (*www.psychcentral.com*), he writes a section called "The Connection Between Mental & Physical Health." In it, he emphasizes that "You'll find hundreds of such studies demonstrating the strong connection between our mind and body's health."[5] His site references researchers at Bangor University in Wales who concluded that "resting up" and having "peaceful mindfulness" before a big day of physical activity helps people feel better and last longer during the day.

Keeping physically fit means keeping mentally fit as well.

2. Healthy Emotions, Healthy Mind

Being emotionally fit improves your self-confidence because you limit the amount of stress that impacts your mind and your body. A commonly accepted definition of stress is that it occurs when a person perceives that "demands exceed the personal and social resources the individual is able to mobilize."[6]

Stress occurs when people feel threatened by a situation. These individuals believe they are incapable of dealing with the particular stress. The amount of stress depends on the amount of damage people believe the situation can cause. Intense stress can cause unhappiness and undermine your self-confidence.

Keep a journal to document your feelings, analyze your thoughts, and record your progress. If you do not like to write, verbalize your feelings. At night, before closing your eyes, allocate five minutes for analyzing your day, highlighting the ups and downs. When you identify stressful situations, you can determine how better to deal with them. For example, if the stress is between you and a loved one, find ways to communicate with this person, rather than bottling it all up inside and letting it simmer. Afterward, let go.

3. Work as a Team

If you have a spouse/partner/friend whom you trust, involve him/her in your endeavors. For example, maybe you have determined that you need to incorporate exercise into your daily routine. Discuss this goal with your partner. Perhaps you can alternate exercising in the mornings while the children are still sleeping. Maybe your kids will exercise with you. Or you can take turns being at home for the kids after school so you can both exercise at the gym. No matter how you resolve your objective of obtaining more exercise, doing it as a team makes the goal more manageable and doable.

And, it can never hurt to have a cheerleader. With one of those on your sidelines, your likelihood of success increases, as does your self-confidence. So list your accomplishments, revel in them, and be proud of them. If you come home and are demoralized on a daily basis or are being limited (for example, being told you can't do something), your confidence will be limited as well.

4. Value Yourself Regardless of Your Job, Salary, or Other Arbitrary Measures

Valuing yourself based on your career is a self-worth trap into which many women (and men) fall. This happens because their personal value is directly correlated with their income level; the higher their income, the higher their self-worth. Self-worth becomes about dollar signs. Then, when you believe you are underpaid or undervalued, your self-worth diminishes.

Your self-worth should comprise a combination of multiple factors, experiences, values, and emotions. It cannot be based solely on money, prestige, or what you do.

Fortify your self-confidence.

Remind yourself of your accomplishments and career aspirations.

Focus on the goal. *Your* goals.

Don't allow Bigfoot to exist.

Don't Mind the Gap

In London, signs advising "Mind the Gap" remind commuters that there is a gap between the platform and the tube. In other words, *don't fall in*. The same holds true here. Previously, I discussed how women negotiate against themselves by assuming what the company can—or will—pay. If a woman makes $140,000 and receives a promotion, she may *want* $165,000 but would accept $150,000, and that spread gets communicated (either verbally or nonverbally). The rationale is predicated on beliefs about the company and what the woman believes other colleagues receive or what the company will pay. On the other hand, if a man earns $140,000 and receives a promotion, he *expects* $165,000 and will push until the company antes up. The man does not care what other people receive.

The difference lies in *expectations*. Men do not *expect* the gap to be a problem. Women do. Therefore, *don't mind the gap*. Don't let a perceived gap inhibit your ability to earn more. If you inherently wonder whether your pay lags behind the market, you will constantly be disappointed. And perception = reality. What you believe on the inside mirrors what you convey on the outside.

Do not expect Bigfoot. If you don't expect it, you won't find it. Don't make a perceived compensation gap a self-fulfilling prophecy. Refrain from negotiating against yourself before even starting the conversation. I have partnered with wonderful, experienced, accomplished female powerhouses who will think up every possible scenario in a negotiation—and what they will accept—before the negotiation even occurs. These women will determine the base salary they would like to receive, but also what they are willing to accept or negotiate before the discussion begins. They assume what the company will be willing to offer without actually hearing the offer. The compensation discussion then becomes a self-fulfilling prophecy.

Don't predetermine the end result. Take the discussions one step at a time. The sky's the limit. Don't put the cap on it yourself.

Do you still think a gender gap exists?

To recognize whether or not you believe a gender gap exists, answer these two questions:

1. Through watercooler talk, have you learned you are underpaid relative to your peers? Do you *think* you are underpaid relative to your peers/colleagues?

2. If you aren't privy to what the top executives earn (male or female), why might you think there is a gender gap? Have you heard rumors? Do you know of three or four women who are high-performers yet consistently paid less than men? Do you know this for a fact?

Typically, the answers are based on personal experiences. Did you find out you were paid less than someone else? Was that someone male or female? How did that make you feel? Did you ask for more money and was denied? Or worse, did you never ask at all? If you believe the company can't—or won't—pay more, ask why. Were you told that before? Or did you think they *shouldn't* pay more because of the current financial situation or a pending business situation like a strategic merger, acquisition, or divestiture?

The key to determining whether an *actual* gender gap exists lies in consistency. Women can—and should—be paid less than male counterparts if they are new to the role, inexperienced, or underperforming. Men can—and should—be paid less than female counterparts if they are new to the role, inexperienced, or underperforming. Remember, a gender gap only exists when women are paid less than their male counterparts *for the same role and performance* (all else being equal).

Another way of gathering intel regarding your company's approach to compensation lies in dissecting the organization's structure. Does the head of HR report to the CEO or COO? Or is the head of Finance or Legal ultimately responsible for HR? Is the head of HR included in all strategy and critical business meetings? Is HR viewed as a critical business partner within your organization? Companies who focus on human resources and treat human resources as true business partners generally do not have gender gaps. The gender gap is more likely to occur in companies without HR, without a critical focus on culture and performance, and without a mission statement that includes its people. These are telltale warning signs to proceed with caution.

Many times, start-up ventures do not grow an HR organization to control direct costs. In this situation, when interviewing, ask about the company's philosophy regarding pay-for-performance. Try to discern leadership's mission and vision, and how that vision involves its people. Catalog the employees: how many are women? How many leadership roles are held by women? How is pay determined? Does each hiring manager do his/her own thing?

Based on my experience advising hundreds of firms, few companies intentionally discriminate against women in terms of pay. Said another way, most companies strive to implement pay-for-performance systems that are blind to the employee's gender, race, or ethnicity. The

*outcomes are intended to be based on perfor-
mance only. Of course, that isn't quite true because the process has inherent subjectivity and
subconscious biases. But my point is, companies try to do the right thing. Of course, compensation is an expense, and companies try to
control costs. If the company can pay you (or
anyone) less, it will.*

Without Bigfoot tracking you, you will be better able to
negotiate a competitive compensation package. If you believe
in Bigfoot, then you are assuming the company either can't or
won't negotiate your compensation. You weaken your negotiating power. In your mind, you've already conducted the entire negotiation without the other party present. Ever buy a car
from a dealer? Did you go in with a strategy of how much you
were willing to pay? Did you assume the dealer wouldn't meet
your number? If you did, did you then decide your number was
flexible and you would pay more? The same principle can be ap-
plied to salary negotiations. With Bigfoot in the room, women
feel intimidated. They are assuming the company won't meet
their number or compensation objectives. Therefore, they are
willing to accept less (in other words, pay more for the car).

Women also worry about being perceived as greedy. This
perception is partly due to internal fears and partly based on
fact. On more than one occasion, I have encountered women
who shared that men actually told them they didn't need to
pay them more because their husband works, or because they
don't need that much money, or because the offer is at least
better than their current salary so they should accept it. This
approach, in my experience, impacts women more often than
men. Companies rarely tell men they don't need to pay them

more because their wife works. Yes, there are double standards. But you can't succumb to the double standard. Rise above it. Don't fall into the trap. Ignore the bait and ask for competitive compensation based on the job's value and your contributions.

Force these people to perceive you positively. Make them realize you are the best person for the job and they can't let you walk out that door. Make these companies realize they need *you*. It comes down to self-perception and letting go of any grudges.

What about the glass ceiling?

In addition to Bigfoot (a.k.a. the gender gap), there is the supposed glass ceiling. The glass ceiling is the idea that companies select men rather than women for senior-level roles. The question is, what holds women back? Barring a few sexist men, I believe we hold ourselves back.

Companies are structured as pyramids or sometimes ovals. As you climb up the corporate ladder, positions become single-incumbent roles rather than multi-incumbent roles as there are at the entry levels. Consider an accounting department. Several entry-level accountants may be hired, but only one or two accounting managers are needed to oversee the group. At the top, there is only one CFO. In other words, you need more worker bees and fewer queen bees to get the job done.

The glass ceiling presumes that men deliberately select only men, rather than women, for leadership roles. However, as individuals progress through an organization, there are fewer senior-level jobs but significantly more competition for those jobs. And, because women sometimes leave the workforce (whether short- or long-term), there are, by default, more men than women vying for these jobs. Consider the number of female CEOs. The competition for these roles is fierce and cutthroat.

In January 2014 the Catalyst organization published a list of women who currently hold CEO positions at companies that rank on the most recently published Fortune 1000 lists (the Fortune 2013 list).[7] Women currently hold 4.4 percent (or 22) of Fortune 500 CEO positions and 4.5 percent of Fortune 1000 CEO positions. The next 500 companies (Fortune 501 to Fortune 1000), in terms of size, currently entertain an almost equal number of female CEOs (23).

Does that mean that women are being treated unfairly? Are women being squashed by a glass ceiling?

Investment firm NerdWallet examined CEO compensation at half of the Fortune 1000 companies and learned that female CEO compensation exceeded median compensation for male CEOs by 13 percent in the most recent fiscal year. The study reported that "Nineteen female CEOs of S&P500 companies earned median compensation of $11.1 million while the 481 male CEOs earned $9.8 million median compensation."[8] Here is another important finding: of the CEO pool, there are superstars. Both male and female. And these superstars earn *amazing* amounts of compensation. Think Larry Ellison ($77.6 million) and Les Moonves ($69.9 million), Meg Whitman ($16.5 million), Indra Nooyi ($17.1 million), and Carol Bartz ($16.4 million). The study notes that the distribution of earnings and people involved is related to the **low level of female participation at the executive level**.

But what do you notice?

The male superstars' compensation far outshines that of their female counterparts. Although women represent at least half of graduates of top business schools, they only hold 4 percent of the S&P500 CEO positions. Very few businesswomen actually become Board members. The NerdWallet study concludes that *the argument could be made that CEO women are actually the right tail of the distribution and are therefore underpaid relative to their right tail male peers.*

Again, does that mean that women are being treated unfairly? Are women being squashed by a glass ceiling? No—not at all. Not one bit. Women need to *pursue* these positions in greater numbers. Women need to be present and actively engaging with men in work and social situations to be considered. No one will know you want the job if you don't raise your hand.

The upcoming female workforce relies on themselves but also on more accomplished women to blaze the trail—both in terms of roles received but also in terms of pay. These female trailblazers not only ignored the gender gap, but they also established new pay heights for themselves and their successors.

In June 2013, Burberry CEO Angela Ahrendts (now at Apple) became the highest-paid executive in Britain, according to a survey from Manifest, a British corporate governance group and pay consultancy firm. She receives 16.9 million pounds, almost 5 million pounds more than the next highest paid British executive—and she is American.

What if Bigfoot really exists?

Simple: If Bigfoot lurks in your office building, seriously consider whether you want to work for an organization that allows Bigfoot to threaten its success. If the organization actively treats women as second-class citizens, ask yourself whether the role will lead to better opportunities or whether you should seek other opportunities. When I see Bigfoot, I run in the opposite direction. If you are in a position to eradicate Bigfoot, then help the organization address a serious issue. Otherwise, look for opportunities where you will be valued.

CHAPTER 9

Rise to the Top

Remember the CFO I conjured in the introduction? How much did your CFO earn? Does that person earn more now? Did you envision yourself in those shoes? Do you earn more now? Do you now know how?

If your primary mission is to increase your compensation package as quickly as possible, then leave your current employer. Today. Joining a new company remains the most efficient and effective way to increase base pay by more than 10 percent. Simply put, companies realize they need to offer a competitive package to entice people to join. Similarly, unless the career opportunity trumps everything, employees hesitate to leave a known situation without being compensated appropriately.

A common career strategy involves leaving, gaining additional experience at other firms, and then returning to the original firm at a substantially increased base salary. Negotiating higher than 10 percent increases by leaving and then returning provides greater compensation increases (over time) than if the person had stayed all long. For example, many consultants pursue "industry" (non-consulting) opportunities to round out their professional experience, and then eventually return to roost, and receive a higher package than if they had never left.

The notion of *having to leave* to increase compensation seems inefficient and ineffective—especially from a company perspective. The opportunity cost of losing employees plus the actual cost of recruitment and training far outweighs the cost of increasing a person's pay. Yet company's struggle with the notion of increasing someone's pay substantially (greater than 10 percent) unless it is absolutely, positively necessary.

Individuals do not want to leave *just* to increase their compensation either, especially if the other rewards and career opportunities prove invaluable. However, an assertive, confident, and politically savvy powerhouse will consider resigning if necessary. Yet leaving simply to increase pay more substantially runs counter to a fiercely loyal powerhouse's need to trust that the company will eventually ante up. However, most companies do not ante up unless maneuvered by the players. Why pay if you don't have to? If you are buying a new car, do you pay the sticker price or negotiate the dealer down? Companies aren't going to pay full price unless it is necessary.

You want to make the company feel it is necessary.

Increase your stock—your intrinsic value by improving how you are perceived.

Be invaluable.

Make the company realize that rewarding you competitively is necessary.

> *I had one dot-com client whose HR executive focused mainly on conserving cost and expense while the CEO and COO were focused on rapid growth and value creation. The HR executive understood the company's business and was acting conservatively; however, the compensation programs that were instituted did not promote the CEO and COO's desires. They didn't share the same soapbox. Fast-forward a few years and the new head of HR (a woman) clearly understood her leadership's mission and openly shared their desires for growth and value creation. She was able to leverage her understanding and successes into higher compensation levels.*

You are the player and *you* need to maneuver the company in the right direction. *You* need to create the results you want. *You* have control over the process. *You* need to play the game and win.

Here is what you need to know *and* believe in order to win:

1. Men are not holding women down or back from accumulating wealth and receiving competitive compensation.

2. Men (on average) are playing the game better than women.

3. It is not about whether Employee A is a male or a female. It is about whether Employee A understands the game, knows how to play the game,

and is *willing* to play the game to improve his/her financial situation.

The Head of HR of a global retail firm understood her relevance and criticality to the firm. She knew that leaving would be detrimental to the company. She leveraged her value and received a highly competitive compensation package.

Yes, times are changing. And women can't wait for companies to "do the right thing." Women need to assume control and direct the outcomes. How will *you* direct the outcome of your personal situation?

1. Ascertain Your Company's Compensation Philosophy

If you work for a public company, read the annual report or proxy filing and confirm your understanding of the company's compensation philosophy. Learn how the company approaches and uses compensation to reward employees. Which vehicles are used, and how? Observe how the company communicates its performance expectations—publicly. If you work for a private firm, peruse the intranet site. Many companies post this information for transparency and accountability. Or schedule a meeting with your manager to discuss the company's philosophy regarding pay and performance.

2. Identify the Players

Considering the industry, stage of growth, and business objectives, which groups influence the way your company approaches pay? What motivates each of these players? How much influence do you—or should you—have in this process (depending on your role)? What matters most to these influencers? How do you link your interests with their objectives?

When I had the opportunity to partner with the confident, yet humble CEO powerhouse, I concluded that not only was her pay below market, but so were other aspects of her compensation and benefits package. There were several items the Board needed to address. Yet she understood the Board and what it was willing— or could—do. This CEO understood that she needed them to be her advocates and her allies first. She was right. It took longer, but in the end, she received a competitive pay package plus a Board that acted with good governance and supported its CEO.

3. Leverage Your Powerhouse Personality

How are you perceived at work? What is your dominant work personality? If you aren't sure, ask people you trust. Which aspects of this personality should you leverage to improve how you are perceived? What pitfalls do you need to avoid?

> *A politically savvy Head of HR powerhouse seemed reticent at our first meeting. She spoke only at certain times. I later realized she was distancing herself from the CEO (whom she recognized would not be long-term) and aligning herself with the right people. When a new CEO was hired, she kept her job and received a competitive pay package from the new CEO.*

4. Play the Game

How should you position your objectives, so that you recognize the motivation of each influential player and improve how you are perceived? How should you become an active player of the game?

> *An assertive Head of Operations powerhouse realized she worked for a high-risk/high-reward firm. She played the game well. She accepted lower cash compensation in exchange for extremely robust long-term (equity) compensation. The company's performance (and her bet) paid off.*

You need to actually play the game to win.

It's like the lottery: if you don't play, you won't win.

And that might be the last stumbling block—actually playing. Some women understand everything that has been laid out, but aren't sure how to jump into the game. The way to start? Network internally. Many women gripe that men are "buddies" because they play golf, go out for beers, or socialize in ways that are less appealing to women. So what? Go play golf! Grab a beer. Put yourself in the same social situations as men. The men won't balk at you. They won't kick you out or run screaming in the other direction. Court clients at hockey and basketball with men, even if you'd rather be watching tennis or baseball. Have a drink before heading home. Don't reject every opportunity to travel. Business travel is tiring, grueling, and unappealing. Yes, it interferes with family time. But a lot of socialization happens out of the office in neutral territory. You don't need to accept every opportunity, but do make yourself available.

If the opportunity to network with Board members presents itself, take it. **Take every opportunity to interact with outside directors**. These directors approve the compensation recommendations presented to them. They need to know who you are and what you deliver. Rather than rely on someone else to communicate your value, do it yourself. No one will sell yourself better than you.

I authored a chapter called "Get a Seat at the Table: How to Become a Board Member" for the book *The Female Leader: Empowerment, Confidence & Passion*, published by the Professional Women's Network in February 2014. I drew chiefly from my own Board experiences, but I also used my networks to approach female Board members to share their advice. Women eagerly supported my desire to provide advice about becoming a Board member. Not everyone I approached was available or accessible for that chapter, but that didn't deter me from my goals and objectives.

Sometimes our fear of rejection precludes us from effectively playing the game. We want to imagine ourselves as top performers, highly admired and revered by our peers. And we fear discovering that we aren't the image we have created in our heads. Women want to know they can effectively succeed at a role *before* starting, whereas men just need to know they have the skills to figure it out. Men don't share that fear of rejection. They are comfortable with learning that there are areas for improvement. They are comfortable because they are confident they can improve or learn a new skill.

Fear of failure is not a reason to avoid playing the game. Fear of rejection should not deter you from stepping outside your comfort zone and reaching new levels of professional and personal accomplishment, including wealth accumulation.

Conclusion

At this point, your imagined CEO powerhouse should be well on her way to earning a comprehensive and competitive compensation package. This CEO should be earning a highly competitive base salary, annual incentives, and other rewards such as equity or retirement benefits.

The sky's the limit.

Make others see you the way you see you—as a powerhouse.

Rise to the top.

Notes

Chapter 3

1. "2012 Say On Pay Results," SemlerBrossy.com, September 2013, *www.semlerbrossy.com/sayonpay.*

Chapter 4

1. "The Wow Factor: Impressive Job Candidate Qualities," CareerBuilder.com, August 2, 2011, *www.careerbuilder.com/Article/CB-2086-Job-Search-Strategies-The-wow-factor-Impressive-job-candidate-qualities/.*

Chapter 8

1. "Highlights of Women's Earnings in 2012," Bureau of Labor Statistics Report 1045, October 2013, *www.bls.gov/cps/cpswom2012.pdf*.

2. "American Time Use Survey News Release," Bureau of Labor Statistics, Thursday, June 20, 2013, *www .bls.gov/news.release/archives/atus_06202013.htm*.

3. "Census of Fatal Occupational Injuries Summary 2012," Bureau of Labor Statistics, Thursday, August 22, 2013, *https://www.bls.gov/iif/oshcfoil .htm*.

4. Bardaro, Katie, "Women at Work: PayScale Redefined the Gender Wage Gap," *www.payscale .com/data-packages/gender-wage-gap*.

5. Grohol, John M., PsyD, "The Connection Between Mental and Physical Health," February 25, 2009, *www.psychcentral.com/blog/archives/2009/02/25/ the-connection-between-mental-physical-health*.

6. "Stress Management—Start Here!," MindTools .com, *www.mindtools.com/pages/article/newTCS_00 .htm*.

7. "Women CEOs of the Fortune 1000," Catalyst .org Knowledge Center, January 1, 02014, *www .catalyst.org/knowledge/women-ceos-fortune-1000*.

8. "Female Executives Earn 13% More than Men, but May Still be Underpaid," NerdWallet Investing, *www.nerdwallet.com/investing/corporate-taxes/ top-executive-pay/info*.

Index

About the Author

Stacey Hawley is the founder and owner of Credo, a compensation and talent management firm. As a consultant and speaker, Stacey has partnered with thousands of executives, Board members, and HR professionals in companies ranging from Fortune 500 firms to pre-IPOs and nonprofits, all at various stages of growth. Before launching her own business in 2011, she spent 14 years consulting for the premier global HR consulting firm, Towers Watson, in its world-renowned executive compensation practice. It was during this remarkable experience that her passion for women's pay blossomed. Interacting with female powerhouses at these firms inspired Stacey to help other women learn how to advance their careers and maximize their compensation. Her advice and articles are featured on national media Websites and publications such as *Fast Company*,

MSN Careers, CareerBuilder, the *Chicago Tribune*, AOL Careers, Monster.com, *US News and World Report*, and The Ladders. A noted writer, she also has articles published by other news outlets such as *Forbes*, BusinessInsider.com, LearnVest, and The Glass Hammer, a leading business blog for women. Stacey writes for *Working Mother* magazine and blogs regularly for WorkingMother.com.

Stacey enjoys life with her husband and three children. You can reach Stacey through her Website, *www.thecredocompany.com*.